Love Israel, Support Palestine
An Israeli Story

Nir Avishai Cohen

D1227458

Dedicated to all people living on this piece of land,
from the Jordan River to the Mediterranean Sea.
In hope and yearning for a life of peace and love.

Contents

Prologue

In recent years, especially since my face has become recognizable in public, I find myself being asked the same questions over and over. The same questions repeat themselves at every lecture, when talking to young people, highschoolers, pre-military academy cadets, and people who are fresh out of the army. After giving the same answers thousands of times, I realized I should probably do it in an orderly fashion, in writing. That's how the idea of this book was born.

Each has a way of asking that question, some direct while others squirm around it. Some can't seem to find the words, while others know exactly what to say.

"Having been brought up the way you were, how did you become this way?" While speaking to them, I often try to linger on the meaning of 'this way' and ask: *What do you mean when you say I am 'this way'?* Then they start squirming. Some say it directly: "How did you become an 'anti-Zionist'?" Others will say" "How did you become an 'IDF[1]-hater', and snitch

---

1   IDF – Israeli Defense Force, the military entity of the State of Israel.

on our soldiers at The Hauge[2]?" Some plainly reply: "How did you become someone who has such different views?" Yes, this is how it is nowadays in large parts of Israel: if you're not part of the mainstream, you're automatically a Jew-hater and an enemy of your country. Add to that a lot of incitement and false information about me personally on social media in recent years, and here are the results.

I'm constantly amazed by people who turn eighteen, having graduated from the Israeli educational system, lacking knowledge of the Israeli-Palestinian conflict. There's no doubt it's not their fault, they are a reflection of what they've been taught and raised to believe. For some time now the Israeli education system has attempted to make certain significant parts of the conflict and its history disappear, showing only one side with a clear and flat narrative, seeking to imprint this upon every Jewish person living here: "They, the Arabs, are the bad guys and we Jews are the good guys." This sentence sums up the narrative. There's no depth to it, no complexity. The Arabs only want to murder us and won't make peace with us, while we Jews constantly reach our hands out in peace and are only protecting the borders of our homelands.

I've met thousands of pre-military academy cadets who invited me to present my point of view. I see this as a real opportunity to have deep and extensive conversations with these young men and women. Time after time, as I meet these young people fresh out of high school and on the verge of enlisting,

---

2   The International Criminal Court at the Hague, Netherlands. The first and only permanent international court with jurisdiction to prosecute individuals for the international crimes of genocide, crimes against humanity, war crimes and the crime of aggression.

I'm amazed by the mixture of slogans the establishment has successfully fed them, a real right-wing brainwashing that sanctifies the settlements, along with something else: ignorance. The less these boys and girls know, the more the system can get the "Arabs are bad and Jews are good" mantra into their brains.

But I have to be honest here, it's not just those eighteen-year-olds, it's most of the country. The right-wing governments over the past twenty years have managed to inject their political agenda everywhere, primarily into the media. Mainstream TV channels start their reports on events in the Territories[3] from a very right-wing point of view, with that same assumption of good and bad. Right-wing people will forever cry out that the media is left-wing since they like to play the victim, but the truth is that the media isn't left-wing at all; like most of Israel, it's in the right-leaning center. I do see the media becoming increasingly right-wing and nationalist, as a result of years-long efforts by right-wing governments.

I stopped in the middle of my life and looked back on my story, the environment I grew up in, the people I'd met, the places I'd visited and what shaped my worldview, creating in me the insights that followed the events I experienced. I'll answer the question of how I became this way in the next few pages.

This is my own personal story, but I believe it contains substantial parts with which some Israelis might identify, each

---

3   The Territories, or the Occupied Territories, sometimes referred to as the occupied Palestinian territories, are the territories militarily occupied by Israel since the Six-Day War of 1967: the West Bank (including East Jerusalem) and the Gaza Strip.

according to their own interpretations or insights that may fit the individual version of their own lives.

Chapter One

Dad Goes to the Army, Actually Everyone Does

One of my earliest memories is from a summer in the mid-1980s, when I was about five years old. It's very hot outside, and Dad's nowhere to be found. He's left for the Reserves. Again. My hero father, with his red paratroopers' army boots, goes to the army quite often. It's an issue during mango picking season, and Mom takes me and my big brother to pick the ripe mangoes. We drive out to the field in our old grey Volkswagen Transporter that fidgets all the way to the family's mango orchard. The road there is paved with prickly Syrian mesquite thorns, and we make our way on foot. I don't remember the actual picking, but I do remember the mesquite. I also remember Mom actually explaining to us that there was no one else to harvest, since Dad was in the army, so five-year-old me and seven-year-old Yuval would get to work. It seems this is where my IDF-related memory begins. Many would probably also say that this is where my commitment to the Reserves began, leading to the fact that I still wear the uniform to this very day, and serve in the Reserves just like my father did back in the '80s. This is where I grew up.

Moshav[4] Almagor was a small place back then, consisting of a mere fifty families, all farmers, all mostly growing mangoes. It was before the age of the Internet, we only had one TV channel, and it mostly seemed like everything was distant from us. This was one of the emotions I remember from back then. Unlike today, in the '80s and '90s, you acquired most of your values from your family and close environment, meaning your moshav friends and your school. The media didn't influence us as much back then.

My grandma came to Israel from Hungary after surviving the Holocaust, at Auschwitz concentration camp. She and her brother were the only ones to survive the Nazi atrocities while the rest of their family was murdered. She made Aliyah – immigrated to Israel – on the *Lo Tafchidunu* ("You Won't Scare Us") immigrants ship. There's still video footage of the ship, in which you can see my grandmother as it docks on the shores of Israel. When she arrived in Israel she met my grandfather, who was also from Hungary and also a Holocaust survivor. My grandfather fought in the 1948 Arab-Israeli War [5] a few days after arriving in Israel. Together they had three kids: Yeshayahu (Shay, my father), Yossi and Esther (deceased). My father served as an officer in an elite reconnaissance unit during his regular service[6], and spent many more years in the Paratroopers

---

4   Moshav is a Jewish type of Israeli town or settlement, in particular a type of cooperative agricultural community of individual farms.

5   The 1948 Arab–Israeli War was a conflict between Israel and neighboring Arab countries, breaking out one day after the State of Israel's Declaration of Independence.

6   Israel has a mandatory military service for both men and women who turn 18.

Brigade's Reserves force.

Yossi and Esther were also officers in the IDF. In 1976 Esther was KIA during her service as a Liaison Officer, leaving my dad's family bereft. One very strong childhood memory of mine is of the family gatherings with my grandparents (long since passed), around Esther's grave on Memorial Day for the Fallen Soldiers of the Israeli Wars. I recall Grandma Leah always saying that even though she was religious, there was no happier holiday than Independence Day because nothing was more important than we Jews having our own country. She, who had made the ultimate sacrifice, constantly reminded us that the State of Israel was priceless, and that we should contribute to its security. I couldn't have been prouder when I arrived in uniform to see her, wearing the Golani Brigade badge and that brown beret on my shoulder: *Here, Grandma, I'm also contributing to the country for which you so yearned, for which you sacrificed your only daughter.*

The classic complexity of Israelism also rears its head in a small and distant place such as Almagor, the mix of Memorial Day bereavement and the joy of national independence[7.] Many years later, during COVID-19, Independence Day at the moshav was celebrated in pandemic conditions: all the residents stayed home due to guidelines against gatherings; I volunteered to drive between the moshav houses in a pick-up truck, hauling a cart and handing out beer, hamburgers and ice cream to each family. This wasn't just to make the quarantined people happy, it was also so we could still celebrate Independence Day, "the

---

7 In Israel, Independence Day directly follows Memorial Day, transitioning between sorrow and happiness.

most important holiday of the year" as Grandma Leah used to tell us. We went from one house to another with lots of smiles, happiness and loud music. All the families came out of their homes to greet us with joy and appreciation. The parents of my childhood best friend Gil – Gilush, as we called him – who died during his military service also came out of their home, a moment after Memorial Day ended. They greeted, encouraged and strengthened us. I stood there on the cart, not knowing what to do, whether I should look down or proudly meet their gaze. That short moment felt like an eternity. The sadness for the bereavement and the joy for our independence mixed together into one human and oh-so-Israeli moment. The Independence Day cart, with its flags and music, meets the parents of the Almagorian officer, "The exemplary Israeli," as his father stated each time they visited his grave, the one who's been away from us for too long.

My dad participated in his Reserves brigade's large-scale parachuting when I was in the first grade, and I remember going to greet him at the training grounds after the fact. That's how we were brought up. Even though my father was a farmer rather than an army man, the army was very present in his life; he would serve around 70-80 days in the Reserves each year.

Another testament that fascinated me as a child was the shrapnel in his right leg. I remember looking at where it stayed lodged in my dad's leg for a while, sensing it with my little fingers, and to this day I don't know what actually happened; my father never boasted about his heroic exploits, he preferred to talk about other things. He only said that the doctors advised him not to take it out, and thus he was left with a lifelong military souvenir.

Even prior to that, when I was in my mother's womb, Dad was also in the middle of a long stint in the Reserves, without cellphones and with very little outside communication. When Mom was in pain, the neighbor was the one who drove her to the hospital; Dad only found out when he returned home. A few months later he was drafted to fight in the first damned Lebanon War, leaving behind a wife with a months-old baby at home and another son who wasn't even three. During Dad's stint in Lebanon, Mom sent him pictures of us, his young children. Dad, who was Company Commander at the time, told us he never opened the envelopes. He was afraid they'd darken his spirits, make him think of what he'd left back home instead of thinking about fighting.

My maternal grandfather, the late Grandpa Avishai – who I'm named after – was the Assistant Director of the Meir Shefya Youth Village and later a farmer at Beit Hanania, a moshav between Haifa and Tel Aviv. His wife, the late Grandma Shula, was a teacher and educator.

My parents looked for a moshav to settle in once they finished their academic studies, a place where Dad could fulfill his agricultural dreams and Mom could develop her therapeutic career, first as a social worker and later as a psychotherapist. They found themselves in Almagor, and after a "trial year" they were made members. Agriculture didn't flourish at Almagor in the early 1980s, and families still struggled to find the right crop for them. We had watermelons, melons, avocados, oranges, grapefruits, but eventually, the farmers at Almagor realized that the climate was ideal for mangoes. Everyone at Almagor grew mangoes. Summer was the harvest season, during the school break. That was how I found myself farming from a very young age, both as part of my education as well as a true need on my part. At first, I'd help fold and arrange crates, then I'd help sort the fruit from the orchard. During 7th grade I was sent to 'the front', picking the mangoes themselves. How proud I was to wake up early in the morning, when it was still dark, and huddle next to my brothers – the older, Yuval, and the younger, Ziv – in a wagon hauled by my dad's tractor. And I was that much prouder to come back home in the wagon at midday, having filled it with mangoes. Mango season was a significant part of my childhood and teen years.

As I've mentioned, love of the country was a value of great importance in my family and my environment. They call it 'Zionist leftism' now. Certainly, the most moral of the left, which I'll discuss in the next few pages.

Like everyone else at the moshav, I was also a cadet and later a mentor in NOAL, the General Federation of Working and Studying Youths. The values they instilled in us were mainly love of the land and the importance of defending the homeland. The movement nurtured the myth of "Tower and Stockade[8]" settlements, giving us the feeling that we moshav folks were an extension of this; that we were the salt of the earth, better than others, the cream of the crop.

Who were those others? Anyone who didn't live in the moshavim or kibbutzim. The Arab neighbors we obviously never mentioned. There are many Arab villages less than 20 minutes from Almagor. We'd never go there, I never

---

8   Tower and Stockade was a Jewish settlement method in Mandatory Palestine during the 1930s, as part of the struggle to establish a Jewish state in the area.

met anyone from there. Giant invisible walls were built and nurtured between the Jews and the neighboring Arab settlements. My only encounter with Arabs involved the agricultural workers from the Bedouin settlement of Tuba-Zangariyye, a village fifteen minutes from Almagor. Before the era of Thai workers, dozens of workers from Tuba would come work at Almagor during mango season, a few even worked at the moshav all year round.

Encounters with the Arabs were always employee-employer relationships. Arab workers only worked for Jewish landlords – a true realization of Zionism and the dream shared by the JNF founders, as well as the other Zionist establishments that mostly dealt with establishing the state itself and guaranteeing that the lands of the country would be in Jewish hands.

My dad, a people person raised in Rosh Pina – in the north of Israel – who saw Tuba from across the street, tried to break down those walls. He had true friendships with many of the people of Tuba. He'd come to their celebrations as well as visit casually. He made sure to take us with him when we were kids, to understand that Arabs weren't the enemy. But this was a drop in the bucket compared to the general atmosphere of the society in which I grew up. The walls of separation between Jewish and Arab societies still stand tall nowadays, and might have grown taller. Young boys from Almagor will never meet young Arabs throughout their childhood and adolescence, despite the minuscule geographical distance between them.

We all share the blame for this. Sure, the education system plays a key role, but the people who don't bother changing the current situation are also responsible. **Mountains of prejudice**

and stereotypes can be built on the basis of separation and lack of knowledge, thus maintaining and even expanding alienation between Jews and Arabs.

I was twelve when Israel signed the Oslo Accords[9] with the Palestinians. My entire family was glued to the TV as the agreement was signed between Israeli Prime Minister Yitzhak Rabin and Chairman of the PLO Yasser Arafat on the White House lawn. Tears of joy streamed from my mother's eyes; peace was actually imminent; we could practically feel it. She was probably thinking of the years ahead, when her children would join the army, that this agreement would bring about a much-awaited calm and we children wouldn't have to experience the combat my father had experienced, or endure what their generation had gone through. Boy, was she wrong. In the 1990s, there was a general feeling in Israel that the conflict was about to come to an end, both with the Palestinians as well as with the Syrians. "A new Middle East," as then Minister of Foreign Affair and later on Israeli President Shimon Peres called it.

But at the same time, the atmosphere grew more toxic, as demonstrations against Rabin and Peres became harsher and blunter. In our area, especially the nearby Golan Heights, graffiti started to endlessly appear condemning Rabin, alongside clear calls for his death. Every few kilometers there would be graffiti on an abandoned house or a roadside sign saying, "Death to Rabin" or "Rabin is a traitor". My father was

---

9　The Oslo Accords are two agreements between Israel and the Palestine Liberation Organization (PLO), signed in Washington D.C. in 1993 and Taba, Egypt in 1995. They marked the beginning of a peace treaty between the two people toward fulfilling the right of the Palestinian people to self-determination.

appalled by these messages, and decided to write a letter to the head of the Golan Council. He mentioned in his letter that incitement within the council was running wild, and that it was the responsibility of the head of the council to order the violent writings erased, as a statement of values from the council's leadership.

He never received a reply, even though the writing was on the wall here, in the faraway north, as well. It was actually reality that replied: three bullets into Yitzhak Rabin's back were the resounding reply to his letter[10]. I was studying at the Beit Yareach high school back then, a school mostly populated by children from the Jordan Valley. The school's heroes, those who mattered most were those who got accepted to elite units in the IDF, meaning that they had passed preliminary screening by the Sayeret Matkal (General Staff Reconnaissance Unit) and Flotilla 13 (Navy Seals). The army was the main topic of discussion as early as 9th and 10th grade, long before enlistment was even in sight. The only discussion regarding the army was how much combat you'd see. It was obvious to everyone that they'd go to combat units, despite some having medical profiles that wouldn't allow them to do so. There was no talk of whether or not we'd join the army, no discussion of morality, only a visible competition for who would be the bigger 'fighter'. P.E. classes taught by the legendary and adored teacher Tzuri, from Kibbutz Afikim, were very tough and prepared us for the army way of life. Tzuri would give us running and power drills to do at home, so we'd be ready for the preliminary screenings and also for military service itself.

---

10   Prime Minister Yitzhak Rabin was assassinated on November 11th, 1995, by a Jewish assassin.

Tzuri had honed and precise mottos that were etched into our minds for many years: "Quantity makes quality" was a line that always incentivized us to go on grueling runs, over and over, anything to become the best combatants in the IDF. Every few lessons he'd take us to the fearsome slope outside school, at the entrance to the dock, on the shore of the Sea of Galilee. We'd run up the slope, all 200 meters of it, then walk or jog back down, and repeat. We'd do it for a whole 45 minutes. I'd completed the same exhausting drill countless times on the slopes of Almagor, in the afternoon – I did anything to prepare myself. I could feel Zionism breathing down my neck, spurring me on to grow stronger and more prepared for my military service.

Army-related deaths also made their way to Beit Yareach high school as one of the kibbutz members from the area was killed in the helicopter disaster of 1997[11]. Since then, whenever we arrived at our only hangout location, HaEmek Disco (the Valley Disco), a giant picture of him would be looking right at us. I'd gaze at that picture with admiration, fully grasping the message society had conveyed to me, intentionally or not. *Here's your role model, the good Israeli, who went to a combat unit and died while serving.* Israeli society never misses a chance to nurture this narrative, to reinforce the sense that the highest thing we can be is a fallen IDF soldier, saint-like.

We also went to the army to become "men", part of the initiation ceremony into the masculine world of Israeli society,

---

11   The 1997 helicopter disaster occurred on February 4th, 1997, when two Israeli Air Force transport helicopters ferrying Israeli soldiers into the Southern Lebanon Security Zone collided in mid-air, killing all 73 Israeli military personnel on board.

certainly with kibbutzim and moshavim back then. We didn't deliberate, never doubted it. The more combat-oriented, the better. And yes, we enlisted because we believed we were going to defend our homeland, our beloved country, our settlements and our families. We were the product of an entire system that brought us up to move forward, happy to do battle whatever the cost. School, the youth movement, media, parents and friends – it was clear to all of them that the right thing to do was to join a combat unit. No one asked the serious questions they should have, no one doubted it.

A female friend of mine contacted me a while ago and told me that her oldest son was about to finish high school, and was contemplating whether he wanted to join the army. She and I are very closely aligned in our political views, she even offered her time to help me when I ran in the Meretz party's primaries. She asked me to meet with him, as maybe my perspective would help him make a decision, whatever it might be. We met, he and I with a coffee travel kit, in an unknown magical forest in the Golan Heights. As the water boiled on the burner, he told me about his deliberation, the same I and all my friends had had. He talked about the need for the State of Israel, but at the same time also mentioned the Palestinians' need to have their own state. He feared his military service would cause our neighbors anguish; he was afraid to be a part of the military force that controlled a civilian population for no apparent reason. He talked about beautiful and humane values that he'd probably gained from his smart mother, values of equality and liberty. He talked about violations of human rights in the Territories on a daily basis, by the same entity he was deliberating on joining. He already knew so much at his young age, knew how to make very astute observations. I felt like I was taking a class on the reality of how I should've acted. To think, doubt, and contemplate. I felt honored to sit with that young man, I never got a chance to know any eighteen-year-old from my environment growing up with such healthy thoughts.

I didn't presume to solve his dilemma, and I certainly didn't encourage him to choose one way or another. But I did try to give him some perspective, from the distance of our 22-year age gap, telling him about my contemplations as to whether or not I should keep serving in the Reserves.

When the conversation with that smart and brave young man ended, I wondered to myself how such a discussion had never taken place in the society I'd grown up in. I mostly understood that the society I'd grown up in wasn't as liberal and open as I'd thought.

My older brother proudly joined Sayeret Matkal and later made his way to Golani's elite unit, where he served as an officer and commanded a team of combat soldiers. The IDF was still deep in the Lebanon mud back then, and Yuval spent most of his time in the Occupied Territories of Southern Lebanon[12], engaged in dangerous operations. I worried for him on a daily basis. Each ominous newscast announcing the deaths of soldiers in Lebanon would fill me with fear. I waited for him to get out of there and return home – I feared for his fate. My mother started her activity in the 'Four Mothers' movement during Yuval's service; it was a social movement calling on the IDF to withdraw from Lebanon. On one hand, my older brother

---

12   The Israeli occupation of Southern Lebanon formally began in 1985 and ended in 2000 as part of the South Lebanon conflict.

was fighting in Lebanon, while on the other my mother was fighting like a lioness against the foolishness of him being there. Perhaps this is the best example of the home I grew up in: the most combat-oriented soldier possible on the one hand, fighting for peace and against unnecessary war on the other.

"Don't ask any questions" was the main motif in joining the IDF. We join the army because we have one country, and we have to protect it. That's it, an unwavering fact. I regret that now. I think we have to ask questions, to doubt things.

I believe seventeen- and eighteen-year-olds should have real and honest conversations with their parents about the military service that's right for them; it's certainly a complex conversation that takes nothing for granted. **A healthy society is one that debates, talks about, and doubts everything. But we're a society that needs healing.**

It's clear to me that my doubt is an outcome of turning considerable parts of the Israeli Defense Force into the Settlements[13] Defense Force. Israeli society has to ask itself hard-hitting questions as to where and why the blood of its sons and daughters is being spilled. A messianic, religious minority has been dragging us into this quagmire for the past 55 years, and we're seemingly following this minority like it's the Pied Piper of Hamelin, sending soldiers on eccentric missions, controlling our neighbors, oppressing them. A small and smart minority managed to build a false representation for Israeli society. They've managed to convince us that all the

---

13   The Israeli Settlements (sometimes referred to as Colonies) are civilian communities inhabited by Israeli citizens built on lands occupied by Israel since the 1967 Six-Day War.

Palestinians want is to murder us. It's a propaganda machine of scare tactics that's been running here for years, on high. We're constantly scared into thinking that any minute now missiles will be fired at Tel Aviv from some Palestinian settlement, and that it's not just because of the Settlements. But something just as bad as scare tactics has happened here, a general feeling that there's no other option. We're convinced that we don't have a partner, that there's no other option than maintaining the occupation. And we get used to this crazy notion as the years go by. We get used to the stench of controlling another people, get used to the reality of violence, of course we do, and maybe we even enjoy that set situation in which we're the victims, that same sensation that has followed us for so many years. It doesn't even matter that we have the strongest army in the Middle East, that our economy is strong – we'll forever be victims. Even the false myth that we're reaching out our hands in peace doesn't exist anymore, only the sense that we're all about to be murdered by the Palestinians.

Our parents, the children of Holocaust survivors, were busy continuing their parents' ways, building up this country. More than that, they were busy building themselves back up, constructing their Israeli identities. My parents' generation took a wrong turn at some point, probably due to the trauma of the Holocaust, and sanctified Zionism along with portraying the Arabs as enemies, instead of sanctifying democracy and portraying the Arabs as our neighbors in this conflict. My parents' generation is one of post-trauma. There are many negative side effects to national post-trauma, and one of them is racism and xenophobia.

'Arab' was a curse word when I was growing up in Almagor. It's still a curse word in many places around the country. They've made sure that we fear the foreign Arab, the one living in the village next door and certainly the one living in Nablus or Jenin. The Arab is always mentioned negatively, 'thief,' 'lazy,' 'terrorist' and other such negative stereotypes. We, the Jewish people, who suffered terrible racism less than a century ago, have ourselves become a racist people. Xenophobia is deeply rooted within Israeli society.

Chapter Two

My Turn to Defend the Country,
At Least That Was What
I Thought I Was Doing

I too entered the most combat-oriented unit I could when my turn came – Golani. I started training in the 12th Battalion, trying to be the best soldier I could be. Boot camp was at Bezek Base, which no longer exists (it was abandoned as part of the Oslo Accords with the Palestinians). During the fieldcraft survival week, we slept in an area very close to Jenin, with Palestinian policemen around. I was given the heavy 'Negev' machine gun to master; it was the most coveted weapon back then. I carried it and its ammunition, which weighed a lot, over many kilometers and became an excellent machine gunner. I was an outstanding soldier by the end of my training, mostly due to my endless motivation. We got the chance to be part of the historic evacuation of Lebanon at the end of our advanced training. On our way there I received an excited call from my dad; he, who had fought in that first redundant Lebanon War and was sending his firstborn son to fight on that same soil, was so proud that I was part of the evacuation of southern

Lebanon, which had caused the unnecessary deaths of too many soldiers.

We were a young platoon, barely out of initial training. We had a mission to go into Lebanon and greet the South Lebanon Army[14] soldiers fleeing the terror of the Hezbollah. The sights were surreal: dozens, maybe even hundreds of cars making their way to us, containing the SLA soldiers and their families. They were terrified. In the background, the IDF was firing shells to push back the Hezbollah combatants, a deafening noise. We were to take their weapons and only then allow them to enter Israeli territory.

It was chaotic. Everything happened so quickly. The SLAs were nervous. The number of weapons they carried with them was incomprehensible. We confiscated rifles, machine guns, grenades and so much ammunition from each car – all given to them by the IDF, of course. We stacked the ammunition in an ever-growing pile, forming a small hill. We feared there'd be Hezbollah agents in one of the cars and that they'd try to hurt us, which was why every vehicle was considered suspicious. The inspection process took time, and the line grew longer. They started shouting that the Hezbollah would be coming any moment to kill them. There was clear stress in the air. We went back into Lebanon at nightfall, to hold a nighttime stakeout in case Hezbollah tried to approach the border fence and carry out an attack. It all ended peacefully. The SLAs entered Israel and there were no casualties among the Israeli forces. This was my

---

14   The South Lebanon Army (SLA) was a Lebanese Christian-dominated militia founded during the Lebanese Civil War, operating as a quasi-military force from 1977 until its disbandment in 2000. The SLA was supported by Israel and became its primary ally in Lebanon from 1985 to 2000.

trial by fire on the front.

A few months later I was sent to a Section Commanders course, in the middle of which Ariel Sharon – a member of Parliament and head of the opposition at the time – decided he would enter the Temple Mount, which detonated an explosive powder keg and started the Second Intifada[15]. We were called back to base from leave and we – the course company – were already deep inside the Gaza Strip the following day, at the Orhan post at the Gush Katif intersection. We'd been sent to reinforce a Giv'ati company there. We were 'green' soldiers, shy of a year into our service, in the middle of a Section Commanders course. The post was too small to contain all the soldiers now huddled together. We placed the beds between the room structures of the Giv'ati soldiers, meaning we had no choice but to sleep outside, with a tarp between us and the sky.

After a few hours there, I lay down on my bed to rest for a while. Suddenly, in the middle of the day, we heard an engine roar followed by a deafening explosion from inside. A hand grenade had been thrown into our post. The first few seconds were chaotic. We newly-arrived combat troops didn't really know what to do. They hadn't even had a chance to give us a proper briefing. We jumped into the fortified ditch and mostly tried to catch our breath. We searched for the vehicle the grenade had been thrown from using our battle positions and rifle sights, but it was already gone. It took me a few years to realize that even today, more than twenty years later, this explosion still exists within me. Every loud noise from a car or

---

15   The Second Intifada was a major Palestinian uprising against Israel that broke out in September 2000 and lasted until February 2005.

a door slamming, any surprising noise, makes my heart skip a beat. I contain it on my own most of the time, but I often share the momentary experience of panic with my friends.

From that day on, and for over a month, we experienced attacks on the post on an almost-daily basis. We quickly became accustomed to it and would immediately fire back at the source, mostly towards "Dekalim House" where most of the attacks came from. We also obviously left the post for quite a few patrols and ambushes – death was in the air. There was a lot of violence. I told my parents we were guarding some base in the area, that we'd replaced a force that had fought in the Territories. I didn't want them to worry. One Friday, I wanted to call home and wish everyone "Shabbat Shalom" to tell them I was okay and that they had nothing to worry about. I tried to guess a time when there wouldn't be any firing on the post. I called around noon. The casual chitchat with my mom was broken after a minute. As I was telling her how everything was peaceful, lying to her so she wouldn't be worried, a long burst of gunfire was fired at the post. I hung up and ran to my 'Negev' (machine gun) station and fired back. As I was firing, I cursed at the shooters for attacking while I was talking to my mom on the phone. When I returned home, my mom told me that she'd heard the shots, was obviously horrified, and had mostly been left with her natural motherly fear, the one that accompanied her throughout the service of each of her three sons. My mom, who shares her life with my dad – whose family, in turn, had already felt the hand of death at their doorstep – had feared the worst.

After 35 days in Gaza, we were replaced by another force, so we could finish whatever training we had left in our Section

Commanders course. A military-grade truck arrived on the day of the switch, to load our equipment; as they were loading the things onto the truck, a Palestinian boy riding a bicycle arrived at the neighboring post (about a kilometer away) and detonated himself at its entrance. No one was hurt other than him. As we took our duffle bags off the truck, we noticed they were filled with human blood and remains. We were all overwhelmed with a sense of disgust.

After that stint I got to command a Golani recruits' section, then I left for an Officers' Course. When I returned to the battalion, this time as a young officer, I once again commanded a platoon of recruits. I felt great pride wearing those brass, officer ranks and the Golani tag, and obviously that brown beret as well. The challenge of commanding a platoon of recruits in the Golani was immense, and I gave it all I had. I tried being the best platoon commander I could, and transformed my platoon into a fighting bunch that would go on to guard the borders of the State of Israel.

I'd engrained the creed to my soldiers on our nighttime journeys, one of the love of the land, preached to the importance of defending the country, educated them to be proud of the fact they'd soon be defending the country and got to safeguard our only country. At the end of the advanced training, my platoon was chosen best one in the base, and I was so proud. I wholeheartedly believed I was training a platoon that was about to defend their country's borders, that I was following my father's and my grandfather's footsteps. Another link in the chain that defended our little country.

One evening, during advanced training, all of us platoon

officers sat down for yet another long meeting that lasted deep into the night. Suddenly the Company Commander (our superior officer) received a phone call informing him of a terror attack near a Paratroopers training base, a few kilometers away from us. He didn't hesitate, and we all went there immediately. As it turned out, a terrorist had arrived at the training grounds, located one of the platoons that were training and sleeping in the field, and opened fire on them. Some of the soldiers were wounded. The soldiers were busy carrying the wounded from the scene as we arrived. We immediately joined them and carried the stretchers up the mountain. We later learned there was also one casualty in the incident, the platoon commander, a friend of mine from the Officers' Course who had commanded a Maglan recruits' platoon. That friend wasn't the first from that Officers' Course class to be killed, and unfortunately not the last either.

We joined the battalion following a six-month training period. These were the days of the Second Intifada, following Operation Defensive Shield[16]. The battalion was deep in operative action in the northern section of the West Bank, around Jenin. My platoon was stationed at the Kadim post, our base of operations. We quickly got into the action. We'd often go into Jenin in our armored vehicles, called *Achzarit* ("cruel" in the female singular form), drive down the streets, make sure the perpetual curfew on the city was maintained. The streets were empty, everyone was indoors. We were occasionally met with gunfire, and we'd fire back at the houses, mostly not identifying the source. *Achzarit* doesn't have wheels but continuous tank

---

16   Operation Defensive Shield was a large-scale military operation conducted by the Israel Defense Forces, from March 29th to May 10th, 2002.

treads, it's a very cumbersome vehicle and every drive down the street would wreak havoc on the roads and squares, as well as the cars parked on the sides of the road. We didn't do any of that on purpose, we just drove down narrow streets. One time, the Company Commander ordered me to make sure the curfew was upheld, and everyone was in their homes. On the outskirts of the city, I noticed a group of farmers working in a vegetable patch. I was sealed away in the *Achzarit* without a PA system. I radioed the Company Commander and explained the situation to him. He repeated his command and told me to find a way to get the job done. I positioned myself with the *Achzarit* in front of the group of farmers, about 200 meters away. I loaded the MAG (7.62mm-caliber machine gun) and fired a few bursts in the air. The bursts made a deafening noise, the farmers knew exactly what I meant and fled back to their homes.

Another time, our mission was to make sure no one left the city. We positioned ourselves in an *Achzarit* on one of the roads around Jenin and waited. Since we were outside of town, we weren't at much of a high risk of being fired at, and we left the vehicle and stood on the road. A few minutes later, an old Palestinian man arrived riding a donkey. He asked to go through to his farming land, I told him there was a curfew and that he had to go back home; no crossing was permitted. He looked at me with a sad, defeated look and turned around. That look in his eyes, his tired and sad eyes, has been etched into my heart to this very day. I felt there was no reason not to let that poor old man through so he could work his land. I thought about my dad, out there in his mango orchard, farming the land without interruption. My heart was torn.

A few hours later we went back to the post. I went to my

room and burst into tears. I think that was the first time I realized how little I believed in what I was doing. I wrote home and told my dad about what had happened, and the thoughts I was having. Itamar – my tentmate at boot camp, a kibbutz member from Beit She'an Valley, my platoon's sergeant, my friend and almost a brother to me – walked into the room and saw me with tears in my eyes. He held me tight and told me he knew how I felt, but that there was nothing we could do about it. "We'll make it through together." Those were probably the most difficult days of my life. **I felt, deep down inside, that the two core values I was raised on were being trampled. These two core values didn't exist in Jenin of 2002. My military actions had nothing to do with my love of the land, and certainly not with my love of people as they are.**

I was torn between my commitment to my men – the ones I'd trained for six months, making sure to get them 'galvanized,' convincing them it was our turn to defend the motherland – and my disbelief in the road we'd taken, the terrible and heart-wrenching daily activity. That night, I contemplated what would be the right move. I knew I had long months of warfare in the Territories ahead of me, that it was only the beginning. After a sleepless night and many tears, I made the decision to stay on; I couldn't forsake my men, who were like my own children, even though I was only about two years older than them. I realized that to be able to do my job, I had to detach "Platoon Commander Nir" from "Civilian Nir." I disconnected myself from my life back home. I didn't go on leave as much, broke up with my beloved girlfriend and hardly talked to my family members and friends. I was just "Platoon Commander

34

Nir." Nowadays, at my age, it's hard for me to understand that decision to detach, and it's even harder for me to understand how I managed to withstand it for so many months.

The next few months were packed with operations, including patrols, stakeouts, many curfews and of course actively defending the Settlements. At a certain point, my platoon was transferred to a post within the Palestinian village of Baqua ash-Sharqiyya post, a village right on the Armistice borderline (also known as the Green Line), next to the Israeli city of Baqa al-Gharbia. When the Battalion Commander visited the post, I was told my platoon would shortly be given the most coveted operation: making arrests. I saw it as the Battalion Commander giving me and my men a vote of confidence. The only problem was that I'd never practiced arrests with my men before; we hadn't run that combat technique during training. I updated the Battalion Commander on the issue of our qualifications, and he looked at me and told me to leave the post with him for a minute. We both stood outside the post, with Baqua ash-Sharqiyya to the east of us, just a few meters away. The Battalion Commander pointed at the houses and told me: "Nir, look what a playground you have here." And I understood exactly what he meant.

The following day, I gathered the platoon together and told them we were going on a training mission. We'd be practicing how to make arrests properly. After I taught them the correct arrest technique, we left the post in two columns. We obviously had Kevlar vests on, helmets on our heads and weapons in our hands.

It was noon on a weekday. I went in first, leading the way. The platoon's movement was tailed by Sergeant Itamar, my beloved friend. I chose a completely random house after walking a few meters. I have no idea why I chose it, maybe because it was relatively distant from the others. The siege on the house was completed within minutes, the fireteam reported to me: 'Closed off.' Only then did I approach the front door along with my fireteam, and lightly knocked on it. "*Jaysh*," ("army") I said in my military Arabic. "*Aftach albab*," ("open the door"). The door opened, and before me stood the father of the family, a stunned look on his face. I told him to leave his house with his entire family, a statement that was all demand and command. The father didn't ask any questions or resist. He called his family – his wife and four children – and they all went outside. The little girl had blond hair and a long braid, the face of an angel. I asked them to stand in a row and not move. I guided Sergeant Itamar's fireteam to make sure they weren't moving, and of course to aim their weapons at them. That's the way it is in the Territories, every Palestinian is a suspected terrorist until proven otherwise, no matter their age. This was also what I told my men, the military's operational perception: men or women, young or old – we must suspect everyone.

I went into the house with my unit. I didn't search it, it was only a training exercise after all, and the house's inhabitants weren't really suspected of anything. I went up the stairs to the roof, where I could oversee my men, and made sure they were settled correctly and that their rifle barrels were aimed at the right place. The only thing I said on the radio to Itamar was regarding the little girl with the long blond braid. I asked if he could see her angelic face. He replied that he could. I left the house within minutes and told the family they could go back inside, and that we were done. At that moment I felt like I was the most moral officer in the world; I was proud of myself for the delicate and pleasant way I'd treated the family. Boy, was I wrong. Today I realize that what I did was practicing on a civilian population. In what world do soldiers train on a Palestinian family as if they're practice dolls? What gave me the authority to go into their house? And that little girl, what would she think of IDF soldiers? Did I give her nightmares? I still think about this family twenty years later, and how immoral I was. But I didn't feel that way back then, far from it. I gathered my men, summarized the drill and went on to the next house.

A few days after that drill, we went out for the real deal. The objective was a suspect in a terrorist attack, who according to intelligence sources had a weapon in his house. I studied the traffic route and the house's surroundings well, and of course got my platoon prepared. We went into one of the Palestinian villages in the area called Qaffin, in the middle of the night, in armored vehicles; Qaffin has since grown into a town. That's the way it is, the Palestinian population grows, some of the villages become towns, and in the future even cities. Life is stronger than any military occupation. The Palestinians won't disappear, they're living right here beside us and will continue to do so.

We quickly got out of the vehicles and surrounded the house. Once the fireteams reported back to me that they were in position, I started marching up the street. The village was quiet, and only the barking of dogs broke the night's silence. I once again chose a random house and knocked on the door. My watch indicated it was 2 AM. The door opened and a 50 or 60-year-old woman stood before me. In my broken Arabic, I ordered her to come with me, that I had a mission for her. The military calls it "Neighbor Procedure[17]." I demanded she go into the suspect's house and tell all the inhabitants to come outside. She did exactly as I demanded, and I let her back into her home once she was done. I explained to my men that 'Neighbor Procedure' was meant to protect us, so we won't be in harm's way for nothing, and if anyone were to get hurt it'd be the Palestinian. While she went into the house, we were crouched behind a cover in case anyone opened fire. I didn't see anything wrong with this demeanor, mostly because all the IDF's arrests were made this way back then; it was standard military practice. I later realized what I had actually done was use the civilian population as human shields. Several years later, the Israeli Supreme Court forbade the IDF from using this practice, as it violated the Geneva Conventions that Israel had signed. In other words, it was a 'war crime.' All the house's residents went out and stood in a line. One of them was the wanted man we were looking for. I cuffed him with plastic flex cuffs, wrapped a piece of cloth over his eyes and took him with us. On the way back to the post, I noticed something about my men, they wanted to get close to the Palestinian and explain to him – with more than just words – who the boss was. I quickly understood that I couldn't leave them alone with him. When we arrived at the post, I released everyone to their beds and stayed there to guard him until the Shin Bet[18] people came and took him away. Once again, I felt like the most moral officer in the world,

---

17   Neighbor Procedure, or Prior Warning Procedure, was an IDF practice during the Second Intifada in which a neighbor or relative of a wanted individual would knock on the former's door and ask them to surrender.

18   Shin Bet is the Israeli Secret Service (ISA), commonly known in Hebrew as Shabak.

even though a minute earlier I'd used an innocent Palestinian woman as a human shield. But this is the way of morality, we can pick and choose.

One of our main operations was to form surprise checkpoints. The military idea behind these random checkpoints was to create a sense of 'haunting' in the Palestinian population. I told my men we wanted to make the Palestinians understand that the IDF is everywhere, all the time. We formed checkpoints that would randomly search passersby to make them confused and scared, which would minimize terror. We called it 'disrupting routine.' And so we'd form these checkpoints throughout the entire day. We'd place the jeep in the middle of the road, sometime a main road or a road connecting two villages, and we'd lay out spikes and start checking the vehicles that passed by. When a vehicle arrived, we would signal from afar for it to stop. Once it was stopped, the mission commander would approach the vehicle while the rest of the fireteam aimed their weapons at the people within. I'd sometimes ask the driver for the passengers' IDs and report them to the post's war room over the military radio. A few minutes later I'd get a reply that the passengers were 'clear,' and I'd let them move on. We sometimes conducted a more thorough check, which meant taking everyone out of the vehicle, obviously while aiming our weapons at them. After all, I did tell my platoon that every Palestinian was a suspect until proven otherwise. We demanded they lift up their shirts, making sure they weren't hiding any weapons or knives. We would then search the vehicle. I let the people continue on their day at the end of that procedure; I never stopped a vehicle and was asked to detain one of its passengers, the checks were always 'clear.' Always.

The platoon went on a regular mission to set yet another surprise checkpoint during one of those scarce times I was on leave back home, mostly because I had to get some sleep. The mission took place at night. I got a phone call in the middle of the night: "There was an incident," Itamar reported to me. As it turned out, the soldiers hadn't situated themselves in a visible spot for the drivers, and a vehicle had suddenly come out of nowhere and kept driving as they signaled it to stop. The driver noticed them too late, the soldiers thought it was a terrorist and opened fire. The vehicle stopped next to them. The soldiers quickly realized it was simply an innocent man who hadn't seen them. He was hit in the leg and evacuated to the hospital in an ambulance. Just like that, a person was shot in the middle of the night.

I went back to the post the following day and looked into the incident. We learned our lessons, mostly how to mark the checkpoint correctly so they'd be visible. The Palestinian? I have no idea what happened to him. No one in the military ever talked about this unfortunate incident or asked me about it. We went on with our very busy routine.

A few days later I once again established another random checkpoint. We suddenly noticed a figure running down the road towards us, a few hundred meters away. We immediately recoiled and cocked our weapons. I noticed a Magav[19] jeep up the hill, turning the other way, away from us.

We noticed more details as the figure came closer. We heard his voice; he was screaming in pain. His hands were cuffed

---

19   Magav, Israeli Broder Police, is a gendarmerie and border security branch of the Israel National Police.

in plastic flex cuffs and blood was dripping from his head. We freed him from the cuffs and our medic gave him initial medical care. His face was swollen, and he had a severe head injury. The young man said he was from the nearby Baqua ash-Sharqiyya, and that he had been abducted by Magav policemen who had pummeled the hell out of him, using their radios to beat him and then dropped him off here. We called an Israeli ambulance to the post. I managed to order my men at the post via radio to stop the Magav jeep. We went back to the post with that Palestinian guy. When we got there, we saw the Magav policemen standing around, looking confused. The Palestinian identified them immediately; they admitted to doing what he'd said. I told them they weren't going anywhere until their commander arrived. Meanwhile, the ambulance came and took the Palestinian to get medical attention. When the Magav commander arrived, he first went over to talk to them. They were standing a few meters from me, so I could hear them. He told them: "You idiots, how did you get caught? How did you let him see you?" He wasn't even angry about the horrible act, just the fact that they had been caught. It was at that moment I was exposed to the cruel reality of what was happening in my sector. I realized that this incident wasn't abnormal, just the fact that we noticed it, that they'd been caught. No one can possibly tell how many cases like that have happened and are still happening. I stood before them and told them they were a disgrace to their country, that they were anything but combatants because real combatants don't just beat people up. I also told them I would report them. Their Company Commander tried to convince me to let it go, that he'd handle them, but after hearing what he had to say to them, I of course didn't believe him. They came back to the post the next day and tried to reason with me, told me they were sorry and asked me not to report them. I was disgusted by them; I felt ashamed in the face of that innocent Palestinian man. I went to the police station and filed charges; it was very seriously addressed. A few days later, an investigator arrived at the post and gathered my testimony. My men contemplated whether to testify or not; I told them it was their decision, but I believed it was our duty as combat troops to do so. Two years later, I was summoned to a court to testify in a trial against those policemen. I stood on the witness stand, a civilian by then, having returned from my great South America trip. Their defense lawyer basically tried to undermine my credibility, and as far as I understood, not very successfully. I have no idea how the trial ended, whether they were convicted or not, and if so, what their punishment was. I don't know whether justice was served, but I felt the fact that they were standing trial in civil court was already a kind of punishment.

As I've mentioned before, a few months after graduating from the Officers' Course, a huge military operation called "Defensive Shield" began in the Territories. I was still commanding a recruits' platoon at that time, but some of my friends were already commanders of operative platoons and took part in the long and violent operation. The nature of warfare is that whoever heads up the force is usually the one who gets shot first. My friends from the course who were platoon commanders were on the front line. They were also the first to die. Six officers from that course died during the Second Intifada, some of whom were very good friends of mine, who had shared a room with me for eight months, while others were 'just' friends of mine from that course. I went to all their funerals; I'd known them well. Each funeral chipped away at my heart a bit more. Another friend dead, another broken family. I'd go straight back to the army after the funerals, to keep serving with my men. I didn't have time to grieve them, not even to visit their families during shiva. There's something unnatural and earth-shattering for anyone, especially a twenty-year-old, losing so many friends in such a short time. I once said that I didn't want my kids to go to their friends' funerals as if they were meeting for beer on a Friday evening. That was how I felt during those terrible funerals. All the friends from that course would meet, hug, exchange experiences and then go back to their units.

Right towards the end of my platoon's course, we took part in an operation at Nablus with the entire Golani Brigade. My platoon was stationed along with a tank company. Our mission was to scour one of the commercial zones of Nablus. We had received intelligence that there was an explosives lab in our sector, but we didn't know exactly where it was hidden.

The streets were empty, and we moved on foot as the tanks drove alongside us. We went through one house at a time, breaking down doors, sometimes using crowbars while detonating them with explosives other times. After quite a few hours of scouring we decided to start setting up sleeping arrangements. I found a sewing workshop that was obviously deserted. Nablus was under curfew, no one was allowed to leave their homes. We settled inside the structure, and I briefed my men on two guarding positions to be manned while we slept. The structure was dirty and quite run-down, and I didn't feel like we were damaging anything by sleeping there. During the briefing, I told the soldiers that we were only here for operational purposes, and so we would not touch or use anything that wasn't for the purpose of the operation. The order was mostly crucial for the electrical outlets; I forbade the soldiers from charging their phones, since it had nothing to do with the operation. I felt a slight resentment, but their reverence of their commander prevented them from arguing with me and they accepted it. We resumed our scouring the next morning and found the explosives lab a few hours later. It was located on the third floor of a five-story building. Senior-ranking officers and Engineering Corps forces arrived right after I reported its discovery. The officers decided to not only blow up the lab, but the entire building. It took the Engineering forces over an hour to lay down the military-grade explosives while we secured the building from the outside. When everything was ready, we moved back to the end of the street and the countdown began. There was a deafening noise at the time of the explosion, sending aftershocks through the entire city. The lab exploded and the entire building went crashing down with it.

At the end of that day, we left the tank company and returned to our own. I received a destination location where the Company Commander and the two other platoons were waiting. To my great surprise, it was a hotel. I had a pit in my stomach going in, a combatants' company inside a hotel. I wondered why the hell we'd assembled there of all places. I gathered my men and told them nothing had changed as far as I was concerned, we wouldn't use anything not for operational purposes. We'd sleep on the floor, in our sleeping bags, and continue not charging our cellphones. One of the soldiers raised his hand and asked to speak. He said that even the Company Commander was sleeping in a bed and using the sockets, as were the other two platoons. I immediately told him I didn't care; I felt my men getting disgruntled but decided to stick to my guns.

A few years later, I met some of the soldiers who were there with me; they reminded me of that hotel. They admitted they'd been just about ready to kill me back then, but in time they realized it had been the right decision.

The brigade-wide operation ended after another day in Nablus, and the company had to leave that hotel. Only then did the other officers tell me that a Palestinian family had been locked in one of the rooms. The father was the hotel's janitor and was there with his family. I was the last to leave the hotel, after releasing the family from that forced incarceration. They'd been in their room for three or four days, and seemed frightened. One of the section commanders made sure to provide them with food and drink while they were locked up. Just before I realized how brutal that actually was, I asked to have a few words with that Palestinian. I told him I was sorry for the last few days, and that I'd come back to this hotel as a guest one day. This still remains one of my dreams, to this day. I can't remember the name of the hotel, but staying there as a civilian would serve as some sort of closure.

Months went by and the Golani course ended. After over a year of training and a lot of heavy operational activity, the course was finally over. The platoon disbanded and I was left without a platoon or soldiers. We'd been together in the Territories for six months, a very eventful, very violent six months that probably left insights within me that will affect me for the rest of my life. The Battalion Commander called me over to talk about my next role. I'd just finished my three years of regular service and had at least one more year of service since I was an officer. He wanted to promote me to Deputy Company Commander and go to a Company Commanders' course. I, on the other hand, told him I needed some air and asked to be assigned to an instruction role. The Battalion Commander was surprised and asked me why. He pressured me until I gave in. I told him I was rethinking the morality of our presence in the Territories. There was silence in the room, it was just him, me and the battalion adjutant. After a while he said out loud, somewhat but not entirely jokingly: "Wow, I'm relieved. I was afraid you were going to tell me you're gay." He went on to say he was glad I had such thoughts and he now wanted me to say even more than before. I insisted on a training position, so I could still contribute to the military but without warfare in the Territories. The Battalion Commander finally came around and relieved me of my duties. A few days later I was called up to have a talk with the Golani Brigade Commander. This was the procedure, every officer who left the brigade had to go through an interview with the Brigade Commander. Unlike the Battalion Commander, who had fought alongside me, and who knew and appreciated me, I was a complete stranger to the Brigade Commander, just another junior officer in his brigade. The conversation with him was completely different; he was impatient. After a few sentences in which I told him about myself, he told me that he'd heard about me and that I had two options: to stay in the battalion as a Deputy Company Commander or to be immediately discharged. I was surprised. After a few moments of thought, I looked him in the eye and told him that if those were my options, I'd rather be discharged.

The Brigade Commander didn't really know how to react, he made the mistake of thinking his threat would destabilize me. "You're not worthy of the brown beret," he told me, and concluded our conversation. That last sentence of his echoed in my ears long after that talk. After three years in the Golani Brigade, a combatant, commander and outstanding officer, the Brigade Commander told me I was unworthy of the Brigade's brown beret. I hadn't been insubordinate; I'd fulfilled all my roles as best I could. All I did, after three years, was ask to do something else while still giving of myself, just not within the Brigade. I went back home with that insult and awaited my discharge. After about a week, I received a phone call from a senior officer of the Ground Forces. He told me the Brigade Commander's recommendation to discharge me had been rejected, and invited me for an interview to place me in an instructor position. A few years after the talk with that Brigade Commander, he was dishonorably discharged from the IDF, after an investigative committee stated he had "transgressed base norms, exemplar, discipline and reliability." I was already a civilian at the time that affair came out, but I felt justice was served and that person – who I'd detested since that talk – got what he deserved, his true colors and values exposed.

During my last year of service, I was the Head of the Patrol Department at the School for Infantry Corps Professions and Squad Commanders, a department that was in charge of instructing and training all patrol sections of the IDF's Infantry Corps battalions. I was discharged from the army after four years and a month, a complex and difficult service that included many physical and emotional challenges, packed with operational incidents – almost all of which had taken place in the Territories: Gaza Strip and the West Bank. During my service, I'd seen death, wounds and blood with my own eyes. I'd experienced fear and pain but also a lot of pride and respect. I was released with a great sense of pride, that I'd contributed to the country's defense, cashed in the education I'd received as a child, without asking any questions. I hadn't yet realized my affair with the military was far from over, and there were still many years of Reserves service ahead of me, which I still do at the time of writing these lines.

The day I was discharged, my mom also "graduated" from six straight years of Yuval and I being in uniform. To mark the occasion, we gathered the entire immediate family for a toast. It was only then that my mom told us that every night – every single night – she'd hear a vehicle driving down the street, she'd wonder if it was making its way to her, bearing bad news. She would only go back to sleep once a few minutes passed and there was no knock on the door. It was then I realized how much she'd carried around back then, how constant her fears and worries had been on a daily basis. I tried to hide my tears, but couldn't. Her nightmare resumed three years later, as my youngest brother Ziv joined the Combat Engineering Corps and also became an officer, serving in the IDF for four and a half years. **My mother was 'enlisted' for over ten years, sending her dearest children to the IDF's forefront, to all these wars she didn't believe in at all.**

Chapter Three

Released, Not Just from the Army

Eight days after I was discharged, I was on a plane to South America, my first destination being Argentina. More than wanting to travel and discover the distant and fascinating continent, I felt I had to get some air. After four years and a month of intense, dense, complex and very violent military service, I had to run away. A real Israeli cliché. I flew alone. I was on a trip with dead soldiers on my mind. I started writing whatever was on my mind in a notebook, a 22-year-old kid unloading the experiences and emotions of nearly half a decade onto the page. They were experiences filled with violence, quite a bit of death and mostly a lot of evil and suffering. I still have that notebook, and I occasionally look through it, the insights of that guy, fresh off the battlefield. There, in the north Argentinian city of Salta, I wrote the following in March 2004:

I've been in South America for two and a half months, so far from home, my family, my country. After four years of insanity, of growing up. I've done so much in those four years, but in truth, very little.

It's here of all places, when I'm far away, that I think about everything I've been through, everything I've seen and experienced. The people who were around me. During this trip, I've realized that what the army gave me the most was sadness. Even in my happiest moments here – and there are a lot of them – I look up to the sky and am reminded of all the friends who went away and won't be coming back. A 22-year-old boy with so many graves connected to him.

When I was in the army and another of my friends died, I was sad for a few days and then moved on as if nothing had changed, as if everything was the same. The realization sinks in when I'm here, only now do I understand how big the world is, how much there's to see and do, how sad I feel over my friends who are six feet deep. Here I believe even more strongly how stupid the situation in Israel really is, how we sanctify things that don't hold true value.

I was always certain Israel was an enlightened country, that its population was educated and opinionated, but I've slowly understood the concealed brainwashing every boy and young man goes through in Israel. No wonder our people are so right-wing, in discord, inured to blood. We hear about wars – some ancient, others new – from the day we're old enough to speak. Look at our heroes: brave warriors who followed the sword with distinction. So few of our heroes are spiritual or men of science.

Later on that trip I also wrote:

I have no doubt I'll have to live my entire life with the terrible things I've done there, in the Occupied Territories, in places that weren't ours. I was a complete and active participant in the oppression of a population, a poor and weak population suffering for many years, on a daily basis, living without hope. And whose fault is that? The Jewish people, who suffered so much, who dreamt of freedom and independence, of their own country, for so many years. Look and see, my Jewish brothers, what this people have become. We've become an occupying, oppressing people for whom mercy and compassion are foreign concepts, and all for the sake of a damned piece of land which in the end –however far down the road – won't be ours anyway. We should know better than any that 'no will or emotion is stronger than longing for freedom, that same emotion the Palestinian people so badly wish for and need.

Unlike many, I haven't lost hope that one day we'll stop being an occupying and oppressing people, that one day we'll be rid of that zealous minority and the territories that don't belong to us, and let the Palestinian people live in freedom, and just as importantly that we stop losing our boys.

Now, as I go back and read the things I wrote right after my service, I'm amazed by the insights I had as a man at the beginning of his adult life. They are the insights of someone who'd just served his country, and now examines himself and his people. Things were very clear to me even back then, before the dust of the battlefield was brushed off my boots. I felt I was on a journey of recovery, one undertaken by many young people freshly discharged from combat service. There, between the peaks, valleys and lakes of South America, I could finally unload my opinions.

Those were the days before Facebook and other social media, and there was still nowhere I could publish my thoughts and opinions as easily as I do today. Who knows, maybe some of my words today would've become some viral post, but I did try and publish some of what I'd written. I felt the need to shout out my thoughts about what I think into the ears of Israeli society.

I went into an Internet café in Buenos Aires, where there was exceptionally slow bandwidth. I used a Hebrew keyboard website, typed a long letter and asked to have it published on Israel's most popular news website, in the Opinions section. The headline I gave the piece was "The Cry of the Golani Officer." However, the letter was never published. Interestingly enough, at that time a small organization started in Israel made up of ex-Nahal brigade combat soldiers. They spoke of their experiences during their service, mostly in Hebron. They called themselves "Breaking the Silence" (*Shovrim Shtika*). Our paths would cross many years later.

In my many trips there, or 'tracks' as Israelis refer to them, I had a tradition I tried to keep time and again. At the end of each grueling incline leading to a divine view, I'd sit down, take a tiny booklet of poetry from my bag and read one specific poem, sometimes aloud and sometimes quietly, to myself. I felt that song lyrics were relevant to my situation at the time: in South America, in some of the most beautiful places on earth, living the best and craziest life I possibly could, realizing a dream everyone had during their military service. Each time I dedicated the poem to some of my friends who fell in combat. I sang "He who dreamed" by Didi Menussi.

He who dreamed and his dream remained
He who fought, won't forget for what he fought
He who stayed awake through the night shall see the light of day
He who went away shall never see it again

He who promised has not put down his sword
He who was called, marched in front of them all

He who loved - many loves are ahead of him
He who went away, shall never love again.

And the mountains still burn with the fire of sunsets
And at dusk still blows the sea breeze
A thousand flowers still delight each heart with their bloom
He who went away, shall never see them.

He who dreamed and his dream came true
He who fought till he heard the victory cries
He who went through the night, and seen the light of day
He won't allow for us to forget the fallen

He who made a promise and got to keep it too
He who managed to return from the roads
He who pained, but understood that pain is mute
He won't allow for us to forget the ones who went away

And the mountains shall burn on with the fire of sunsets
And at dusk the sea breeze shall flutter
A thousand flowers shall bloom in and around the trenches
They'll testify we've remembered them all

I felt this was how I was honoring my fallen friends, much more so than the funerals I'd attended. While I got to see "mountains burning in sunrise," I still felt the pain of losing my dear friends. I'd sometimes actually say their names and, as mentioned, dedicate the poem and the stunning view from that spot to someone else. I was deeply moved, feeling a sharp pain followed by tears each time anew. I remembered them all.

I was certain I'd start my own personal fight against the occupation upon my return to Israel.

That didn't happen.

***

Israeli society was hemorrhaging at the start of the 2000s. There were many casualties, civilians who died in terror attacks and soldiers falling in the Territories. The economic situation wasn't great, and the overall atmosphere wasn't good. Many on the political left felt the bad situation would lead to a change, that there were so many signs of that, that they would lead to 'people realizing that peace is better than war. I was one of those people; I thought the public would understand that the occupation is the primary cause of these unnecessary deaths, the spilled blood and the shaky economic, national and personal conditions. It didn't happen. I was wrong. Since then, the occupation has only deepened, more settlements have been formed and our control over the Palestinians has grown harsher and tighter. But something else did happen, the Israeli economy quickly grew and prospered, Israeli hi-tech brought a lot of money into the market and made Israel a wealthy and financially stable country. In addition, there was relative calm in the Occupied Territories. This was true from about 2010 to 2021. Other than specific conflicts, the violence Israelis had experienced decreased significantly, especially for Israelis who didn't live in the settlements but within Israel's borders. Terror attacks in the heart of Tel Aviv became history, and the sense of personal security increased. There's a new generation now that doesn't know the word 'peace', but also hasn't experienced the violence of those damned Second Intifada days.

Once, a long time ago in the 1990s, there was a very popular sticker that read: "An Entire Generation Demands Peace" (*Dor Shalem Doresh Shalom*). A generation of young people understood that our future would be better if 'we had peace with our neighbors, mainly the Palestinians. A generation has dreamed and even talked about not having their children join the army to fight, but only to safeguard the legitimate borders of the State of Israel. This generation is now in their 50s or 60s, their children serve in the army, in those same damn places, having to step into the same places their parents once stepped: the Kasbah in Hebron, Jenin, and other places most Israeli citizens will never visit.

There's an entire generation for whom the word 'peace' is foreign. We've stopped talking about peace with the Palestinians. The most we can do is make peace with the UAE and Qatar, distant countries with whom we've never been in conflict. But far be it for us to mention peace with the Palestinians; this isn't an option. We've been brainwashed to think there's no partner on the other side, that all Palestinians want is to kill us. A child born in the 2000s knows what they believe to be a pretty good situation: a safe country with a great economy. The violence is mostly in the backyard, somewhere in the Territories/West Bank/Judea and Samaria, whatever their names are. Most Israeli have never crossed the Armistice Line and probably will, they have never seen or visited settlements, and certainly not Palestinian villages. It's been years of status quo, and that silence serves those who are indifferent to the Palestinians' condition, and obviously the settlers who continue to expand their presence in the Territories. Israel hasn't done anything of significance in the Territories since Gush Katif[20] was evacuated.

---

20   Gush Katif was a bloc of 17 Israeli settlements in the south of the Gaza strip which was forcibly evacuated in August 2005.

We have to face reality and honestly admit that the settlements damage Israel's security: as long as they exist, we cannot form a real border between Israelis and Palestinians. An army can protect a territory best when there's a clear border, the opposite of what's happening in the West Bank. But additionally, children – our children – get killed in the name of the settlements and Messianism. Soldiers roam the villages and towns, such as Ya'bed, believing they're there to protect their families while the painful truth is that they are pawns in the hands of detached, indifferent and cold-hearted politicians.

It's no coincidence that most generals fresh out of the service talk about Israel's need to create a clear border between Israel and the Palestinians. They understand better than all of us that such a border would reinforce Israel's security and allow the IDF to better defend the country. But we're still there. These politicians still endanger our fighters from their ivory towers, due to that Messianic settlement approach.

***

After the first trip, I went back to work on the family farm, "doing the season" as the locals used to call it. At the end of that season, I went to the States for a few months and from there to South America. I fell in love with that continent, the language, and especially beautiful and pleasant Argentina. After two years of wandering the globe, I finally returned to Israel. I joined the Shin Bet's security array via flight security. I went through their "Achid" course, where we learned to become excellent security guards with nearly impeccable firearms and Krav Maga skills in only three months. I was sent to Cairo, the Egyptian capital, at the end of the course. I worked at the Israeli embassy there, as well as securing El-Al flights to Cairo. I lived in Egypt for a year; an interesting and educational experience. I freely roamed the city, making sure to visit all the museums this huge city has to offer, and of course the impressive pyramids of Giza which I saw from my window in the Maadi neighborhood. It was very interesting to see the Egyptian narrative. October 6th is an Egyptian national holiday, one of the main bridges on the Nile is even named after it, and the luxurious War Museum tells the story of Egypt's glorious victory that day. Something wasn't right for me: Israel was ambushed on October 6th, 1973 – when the Yom Kippur War broke out – but it was Israel who ultimately won the war, at least that was how I was taught to think. I wondered about the Egyptian narrative with an Egyptian scholar who worked at the Israeli Academic Center established in Cairo following the peace treaty, not far from the embassy. That history lecturer explained to me that this war was taught as a great victory for Egypt, for two reasons: first, the Egyptians had managed to greatly surprise Israel and cross the Suez Canal. I immediately thought it was similar to a team celebrating its win at the end of the first half only to lose by the end of the game. However, the second reason was illuminating for me: the doctor claimed that the aim of the war had been to regain control of the Sinai Peninsula that had been conquered six years earlier, during the Six Days War.

"So," I replied, "the Sinai still remained under Israeli sovereignty at the end of that war."

And the doctor replied: "It depends on what you consider to be the end of the war."

While the Sinai did remain under Israeli sovereignty at the end of the Yom Kippur War, four years later the Egyptian president Sadat visited the Israeli Parliament, and at the end of that peace process Israel retreated from the Sinai Peninsula and returned it to Egypt. Does the Yom Kippur War have anything to do with the peace treaty? Absolutely. This is how the Egyptians see the wider context of the war, leading to their regaining sovereignty over the Sinai Peninsula. I was reminded of one of my lessons from the Officers' Course, about the father of modern warfare Carl von Clausewitz who said as early as the 19th century that "War [...] is an act of violence to compel our opponent to fulfill our will," and that "war is nothing but the continuation of policy by other means." This is exactly what happened in the 1970s between Israel and Egypt. We now clearly know that the Yom Kippur War could've been avoided. Before the war broke out, the Egyptians contacted then-Prime Minister of Israel Golda Meir, seeking a peace treaty in exchange for returning the Sinai Peninsula to the Egyptians. Golda refused. The Egyptians started a war that cost the lives of over 2,000 Israeli soldiers and more than 15,000 Egyptian soldiers, with many thousands more injured on both sides. What the Egyptians had asked for, before entering the battlefield, happened several years later anyway. Rivers of blood could have been prevented had Israel been willing to sign a peace treaty with Egypt. Rivers of blood and bereavement could have been averted had the Israeli leader also been willing to extend her hand in peace. How many Israeli youths know about Israel's refusal before the Yom Kippur War? Very few. How many of them have heard tales of bravery from that war? Many. The Israeli education system accentuates values of violence and war for the youth, blurring and almost erasing values of peace and compromise.

***

Living in a foreign Arab city for a year was very significant to me. While we Israelis travel all over the world, from the peaks of the Himalayas to the icebergs of Patagonia, the 'Big Apple,' sacred Manhattan and all those glamorous European capitals, hardly any Israelis visit the Egyptian capital which is less than an hour's flight from Tel Aviv. Sure, they've scared us into thinking Arabs everywhere will murder us. Cairo is a culturally rich and very interesting city, and I consider it a must-visit destination for Israelis. Whenever I was asked where I was from while roaming Cairo's streets and markets, I always replied that I was Israeli. I never encountered a disagreeing face; to the contrary, I was always welcomed. People were curious to hear about Tel Aviv, and obviously Jerusalem. The merchants often wondered why Israeli tourists didn't make their way to Cairo anymore, and why they hardly saw any Israelis. I was ashamed of my reply, but I still said many of them are simply afraid for their lives. Every merchant replied the same: you have nothing to fear, there's peace between Israel and Egypt; besides, it's our leaders' wars, it has nothing to do with us. Later that year, my parents and some of my friends also visited there, all returning to Israel amazed at this special city, mostly wondering how they hadn't visited earlier.

After a year in Egypt, I spent a year securing Israeli flights in Greece. I then worked as an air marshal on the flights themselves for three years. While working on aircrafts, I did my Bachelor's degree in History, Political Science and International Relations at the University. Friends who worked with me in Egypt and Greece offered me a job with them at a mysterious company called Logic. They told me the company was integrating various security systems and mostly worked in one country in the world. Only when I started working there did I realize the country in question was the United Arab Emirates. It was 2010, long before the peace treaty between Israel and the UAE. The client inviting the company was the authorities themselves, who obviously knew we were Israelis and were interested in Israeli technology to defend their strategic facilities, such as oil wells and power and water facilities. Logic provided Emirate authorities with cameras, detectors and other such devices to help protect these sensitive facilities. For security reasons, we'd fly there under non-Israeli nationalities, skipping the regular border control. Most Israelis have no idea that many Israeli companies have worked in the Persian Gulf for many years. These countries never saw Israel as an enemy; on the contrary, they and Israel share an enemy in Iran. I of course welcome peace treaties with these countries (the "Abraham Accords"), but this is nothing like the actual peace treaties signed here with Egypt, Jordan and of course the Palestinians. While there's an importance to the Abraham Accords, the really hard part is making peace with our close neighbors, especially the Palestinians.

Other things bubbled up within me beside the need for employment, such as my love of sports, stamina and especially long runs, like marathons and ultra-marathons – all of which led me to get a teaching certificate and a Master's degree in Physical Education. I left Logic to study Sports for two years. I spent one year at a facility for troubled youth and another as a regular teacher at Tichonet High in Tel Aviv. All in all, my teaching experience was good and educational, but I was astounded by how poorly it paid. Even though I knew how much teachers made, I was shocked each time my paycheck arrived. It was insulting. This paycheck is mostly insulting to us as a society. A society that emphasizes the education of future generations cannot afford to pay its teachers so little. I and the teachers who worked with me had to make ends meet after school. Some of them were private tutors, but others also waited tables or babysat so they could pay their bills, and a teacher who has to work on the weekend instead of resting certainly won't be at their best for the new school week. Israeli society has forsaken the education system, and we see the results each and every day. I have no doubt that more people of high quality and value would've turned to teaching had the salaries been higher. I left the education system because I decided to go into politics at some stage, since the fight against the occupation burned within me. I believe I'll one day return to teaching, given my strong belief in education.

Chapter Four

The Keys to Peace

Understanding the other side is one of the keys to peace. In other words, how do the Palestinians see us, Israelis, let alone the IDF? A fragment of that understanding was revealed to me in 2018. I'd flown to Greece on behalf of an organization that dealt with the Israeli-Palestinian conflict, for a seminar with six Israeli and six Palestinian members. We were all involved in politics in one way or another. The goal of the seminar was to further educate us on the conflict, to get to know and understand the "other side", and to try and come up with solutions. The gap between us surfaced even before the seminar began. We Israelis arrived in Greece through Ben Gurion Airport (Israel's international airport) while the Palestinians, who lived in Hebron, Jenin and Nablus, had to get to Jordan through the Allenby crossing and board a flight to Greece from Aman. The Palestinians lived a short drive away from us, yet what we did in an hour's flight took them almost an entire day.

The seminar started with an introduction as the organizers handed out short biographies for each of the participants. We later had many interesting discussions that also obviously included arguments; all in all, the atmosphere was positive. During the coffee breaks between discussions, we got to know each other even more, and you could actually sense the ice breaking between us. The differences between the two groups were quickly evident. While we Israelis had average English at best, all the Palestinians had excellent English, much better than ours. They all belonged to an upper socio-economic class, and besides being involved in politics they were successful in other areas as well. Some had degrees from abroad or had spent extensive periods of time outside Palestine. They belonged to the Palestinian elite, each in their respective field. We were quite a mediocre bunch, with a lot of good intentions but certainly not the Israeli elite.

The Israeli group included people from the political center, some of whom might even describe themselves as Zionist left-wing. Maybe. I was the odd one out, due to both my knowledge of the situation in the Territories as well as my opinions. I found myself agreeing with most of the Palestinians' claims and made sure everyone in the room knew it. I felt much closer to their ideas than those of the Israelis. My Israeli colleagues didn't really know how to address the fact that I wasn't on their side, but rather claimed the Palestinians were right.

During one of those times, as I was explaining why I thought the Palestinians were right and deserved liberty and their own state, and why Israel is mistaken in imposing martial law on a civilian population for so many years, a young woman – Nadine of Nablus – interrupted me. She stood up and said to my face that my words were meaningless, since I served and still serve in the IDF, the occupying army, per my biography. She all but shouted that I couldn't occupy as a soldier and then argue against it as a civilian: "You're an officer in the enemy's army, I'm sure you've done unspeakable things in the Territories, you are the worst." There was silence in the room, everyone was looking at me. Nadine had confronted me with her point of view, with what she considered to be the painful truth. All her life, the only thing she saw were soldiers preserving and deepening the occupation, she'd seen it with her own eyes and had experienced in the flesh the IDF as an evil army that stripped her of her basic rights and liberties. To her, as she mentioned, the IDF was a cohesive entity whose presence in the Territories was about oppressing Palestinians. Nadine simply couldn't understand how I could have my opinions and still occasionally wear the uniform. Many Israelis feel the same way. To many of them, my Reserves service conflicts with my opinions.

I was surprised by her directness and aggression, but was willing to reply. Nadine sat back down with fire in her eyes, awaiting my response. I stood up and looked into her eyes, feeling that I was only speaking to her and not caring about anyone else in the room. I told her about my grandparents surviving the Holocaust, about my parents and the Jewish people's need for a state. I said I believe in the existence of the State of Israel as a home for the Jewish people and all its citizens, and about our right to defend our borders. Even though many people don't realize it, most of the IDF's activity isn't in the Territories, but at Israel's legitimate borders. When I wear this uniform and serve on our peace borders with Egypt or Jordan, I couldn't be prouder and more complete. This is the IDF's real purpose, to defend, not to occupy. My heart was pounding, and I contemplated whether I should keep talking, finally deciding to go on. I confessed to her that I wasn't willing to serve in the Territories anymore, even if ordered to do so. I can't change the past, but I can take responsibility for it, and I take responsibility for the things I've done in the Territories as an Israeli officer. As a civilian I'm doing my best to change this situation, trying to do all I can so that she and her family can have liberty, so they can have their own country. I sat back down. Nadine didn't respond. The seminar's moderator called a thirty-minute break; Nadine and I didn't speak during that time.

In the evening, we went out to a pedestrian mall near the hotel, with restaurants and bars. We all had some alcohol, and the atmosphere loosened up. At some point, some of the people went back to the hotel, and I went to a dance club with another Israeli woman and a few people from the Palestinian group. We all danced together, as if there was no conflict. We danced as if it could mark the end of the terrible state both our peoples are in. I saw Nadine occasionally looking at me, probably since she noticed I'd been looking at her. With her terribly beautiful features and perfect eyes, she almost hypnotized me; I couldn't take my eyes off her. I could feel the tension between us. Just a few hours ago I had been her greatest enemy, and now we were dancing with each other, growing ever closer. We couldn't deny our attraction any longer, and everyone around us saw it as well. On the way back to our hotel, Nadine and I walked side by side, somewhat speaking, somewhat flirting. Marach, her best friend from Jenin, came up to her and dragged her back. Later, Nadine told me that Marach had really scolded her, telling her she couldn't walk with me like that because I was an Israeli. Nadine had told her that it was obvious to her, and that she wasn't about to act on it, that she had nothing to worry about. We managed to exchange phone numbers before Marach pulled her away. I went into my hotel room and sent Nadine a message.

"Are you off to bed?"

She immediately replied: "No, I'm not tired."

"So what can we do?" I asked.

"We can keep talking in your room. We can't do it here because Marach is in the next room, and I don't want her to hear us."

I of course invited her over. I left the door open so she wouldn't make a noise while knocking. Nadine came in and sat beside me on the bed that filled up most of the room. Before she came over, she'd changed into a t-shirt and sweatpants, which made her seem even more beautiful and attractive.

We were quiet. At some point, I felt as if I were in a scene from a movie, or a chapter from a book. After silence, the words wouldn't stop; we talked for hours, and I drank in each of her words. She was one of the smartest, most intuitive women I'd ever had the chance to know. In a courageous move that took us both by surprise, Nadine decided to spend the night with me. Just before we fell asleep in each other's arms, she whispered, somewhat to herself or to me: "I can't believe I'm sleeping with the enemy." I smiled and hugged her tighter, but deep down my guts churned. I didn't want to be anyone's enemy, certainly not to my Palestinian neighbors. As if we were the greatest cliché on Earth, that night in not-so-distant Greece, two people – an Israeli and a Palestinian – slept together in an embrace, proving mostly to themselves that at the end of the day – and perhaps at the end of the night – we're all human.

We obviously agreed to keep that night a secret, along with the entire relationship we were about to have. In the morning we were perfect strangers again, keeping that wondrous night to ourselves. A few months later, when I visited Nablus with an Israeli delegation, Nadine secretly came to visit me. I left the meeting to enter a nearby stairwell, and she was waiting for me there. I once again felt like I was in a movie. We only had a few minutes together and we mostly hugged; I'd missed her. She told me she'd given up on Palestine, that she needed to get some air, that she felt the occupation weighing down her soul and she was going to go away for a long time, and might never come back. I didn't know what to say other than I understood, and obviously being somewhere else without the Israeli army around would do her good. On the other hand, I didn't want her to give up the fight, believing that someone like her had a great future ahead of her in Palestinian politics. Before we said goodbye, I promised I'd come visit her abroad.

Chapter Five

The Red Lines Aren't Bold Enough

The first time I was called to the Reserves was in the summer of 2005, less than two years after I was discharged. I started serving as a platoon commander at an Infantry battalion. My first stint in the Reserves was just before Israel's disengagement from Gaza. We took over for a Border Police company at Har Harif, on the Egyptian border, as they went to evacuate Gush Katif. I had just arrived in the battalion and didn't know anyone around. I was young, only 24-years-old, and everyone else was older than me, most of them in their 30s. I found out that some of them chose not to do their Reserves stint because they were "angry" at the army for being the entity that practically evacuated the settlers from Gush Katif. There weren't many of them, just a few individuals from each company. I despised them without even knowing them. I thought they ought to be judged for absenteeism and sent to military jail. Even though I was new there, and quite young, I made sure my commanding officer knew how I felt. I also said I think that these men shouldn't serve in the company, and should be removed from the Reserves altogether. I was considered a minority, and not for the first time. The battalion forgave everyone who failed to show up back then, no one was sent to jail and in fact, none of them were punished in any way. The army sold its values for the sake of the settlers and Settlements, and that wasn't the first time either.

A year later, while operating on the Gaza border, all the renegade civilians/soldiers showed up. I was so mad about it but there was nothing I could do. As I continued my Reserves service, two of these renegades became some of my best friends. Later on, as I became the commander of that company, I designated one of them to be a Platoon Sergeant while the other one was an outstanding combatant and was an example to follow. In retrospect, alongside disagreeing with their actions – certainly in the headspace I'm in while writing these words – I appreciate the brave step they took. They were loyal to their values and drew a red line that they weren't willing to cross. It took me a few more years to make peace with the red line of my values. They obviously could've done so and got away with it only thanks to the right-wing atmosphere that dominated the country at that time. Yes, I've learned throughout the years that there's politics also within the army. Those who support settlers are treated leniently and are sometimes even supported by all ranks. And so it is the other way around, there's a strictness to any resistance made to the Settlements and occupation.

During the operational activity at Gaza Envelope, following the disengagement, I already knew my company members well. In fact, I formed another social circle in my life, and it's still with me. Year after year, meeting the same people who wear their uniform and meet, year in and year out, really does the trick; it's a very significant circle of friends in my life.

Something happened during that Reserves stint that overstepped the usual patrols and ambushes.

On one of the nights, our lookout identified two people trying to approach the fence from the Gaza side. I was commanding the company's standby force at the time, so we immediately went there and situated ourselves about 100 meters from the fence. My force had a sniper, who quickly placed the weapon and started looking for the "dirties" – as the terrorists are called on the radio, I guess because they perceived Arabs to be dirty and smelly people. The two individuals walked quite slowly and were very close to the fence. The orders were very clear: any attempt by Palestinians to cross the fence meant the risk of a terror attack, especially at night, and they must be shot. The Company Commander gave the sniper the order to shoot. A loud gunshot sound broke the silence. The sniper calmly said: "One is no longer with us," and reported shooting one of them in the head. He immediately shot the other person as well. They were a few meters away from the fence. The lookout reported on the radio that the first one was lying on the floor, without moving, while the second one was standing with his hands in the air. We quickly made our way to the fence. When we got there, we saw a 17-year-old boy with a terrifying look in his eyes. The sniper's bullet grazed his arm, he was missing a piece of flesh under his shoulder, and he was bleeding. He didn't shout in pain, probably due to the shock and fear. I was the only one there who knew some Arabic, mostly from my year in Egypt. I ordered him to take off his shirt and pants to make sure he wasn't carrying a charge on him. He followed my orders and remained wearing nothing but underwear; only then did we let him cross the fence. The boy was in shock and incoherently mumbled something. The battalion's medic arrived and provided him with first aid; he was later evacuated to be treated at the hospital. The Palestinians reported the first guy as dead. The day after, the Shin Bet representative informed us that the wounded boy we captured had been returned to Gaza. After an investigation, it turned out that they didn't have any terror intentions but were two boys who came looking for work in Israel so they could escape the terrible situation in Gaza. All I was left is the thought of how things must be so terrible in Gaza, that these boys went so close to the fence, in the middle of the night, choosing to risk their lives. One of them paid for it with his life.

Reserves service has become a significant part of my life. I went on four stints with my company within five years, meaning serving in operational sections, each one for about a month. Har Harif, Gaza Envelope, Gush Etzion and Tulkarm. This is a lot on any scale. I felt the strain and, on top of that, we trained quite a bit. The new Reserves Law, enacted in 2008, made the burden of the Reserves more tolerable. The law stated that each battalion would engage in operational runs once every three years and not every year. And that's a good thing.

I was called for Reserves service in the Territories twice. For three weeks in 2008 at Gush Etzion, and three weeks, a year later, in the Tulkarm area.

As I've mentioned before, the conflict of serving in the Territories had been going on inside my head since the day I was done commanding the Golani platoon, but I had to deal with it in reality. I hadn't served in the Territories for five years since, and then I received an order for a spell at Gush Etzion, in the Territories. I was already Deputy Company Commander, socially and ideally emersed into the atmosphere of the company and the battalion. I thought I wouldn't be like those sad sacks who didn't report for their Reserves service during the disengagement, that I'd be a better citizen. Despite my resistance to the occupation, when my democratic country calls, I'll certainly report for duty. This is possibly the essence of the difference between us, left-wing people, and our fellow right-wing ones. No matter what they do, they'll always be defined as Israel lovers, while we – the left-wing people – will have to forever prove our commitment to our country. The right-wing propaganda has washed over us as well. In order to better understand the equation, you need only look at the stone-throwing and violence perpetrated against IDF soldiers by some of the Settlers in recent years and the forgiving treatment these violent factors – and sometimes even Jewish terrorists – receive from Israeli society, certainly from the Defense Forces and government. Compare that to the violent treatment the Defense Forces inflict on the Israeli human rights activists operating in the Territories, when all they wish to do is show democratic solidarity and anything but violence. Those activists are marked as Israel and IDF-haters.

I contemplated what I should do for a while, and finally decided to receive the democratic sentence and if my democratic state sent me to the Territories, I'll go. In retrospect, when I'm much more complete with my views today, I understood I'd made a mistake. **Serving in the Occupied Territories, especially Reserves service, is surrendering to undemocratic principles, and worse, taking a full part in war crimes that the IDF is committing in the Territories on a daily basis.**

I'm not proud of my Territories service, but I'm also not trying to cover it up; it's part of my life story.

My company was stationed at the regional brigade's base, near the Gush Etzion intersection. The section we were trusted with had quite a few Settlements, the largest of which was Efrat. As part of getting to know the section, the Company Commander and I went to each and every such settlement, so we knew all of them. This stint was actually a lesson in expanding Settlements. A sister-Settlement was established next to each regulated Settlement, "an illegal outpost," as the army calls them: several trailers on a God-forsaken hill, but one that has a road that goes to and from that veteran, regulated Settlement. The difference between these settlements was that, while the Settlement was established based on a government decision and with the military's authorization, the illegal outpost was illegally established, without the military or government's approval. However, the military is obviously cooperating with those settlers and guards them instead of evacuating them, even though they're illegally invading land that doesn't belong to them.

Some of the strongholds included three or four trailers and at least four soldiers who had to guard the place, sometimes even more. Our soldiers, Reserves soldiers who joined to guard the country, found themselves guarding a few marginal and illegal trailers, without any fence, while putting their lives on the line. These strongholds grow as time goes by, and their evolution shows they eventually become legal and legitimate as far as the state is concerned. On one hand, the settlers develop the myth that they care for IDF soldiers, giving them candy and cakes, but on the other hand – in reality – they endanger them for nothing. Soldiers' blood is spilled because of that violent, messianic belief. That's the truth.

One of the Settlements in our section was Bat Ayin. We warned that some of the Settlers there are violent and hate the IDF and police. There were cases of stone throwing on IDF jeeps in the past, and we were briefed to stay alert. The Jewish terror against the Defense Forces is part of the reality of the people serving in the Territories. The IDF and police are obviously forgiving, and even ignoring, those violent terrorists.

During the transition period over this section, we were explicitly told that we should make sure the Palestinian and Israeli residents are separated at the bus stops at the Gush Etzion intersection, where our company served. They shouldn't stand close to one another, and each group should be at the place allocated for it at the intersection. Like many things there, the separation was under security pretenses, they claimed that we had to keep the Israelis safe by making sure the Palestinians stayed away from them. The separation of the civilian population was forced by IDF soldiers. Without saying anything about Apartheid.

Three days later, the regional Brigade Commander toured the section with all the Company Commanders and their deputies. The tour included an observation of strategic areas and a surprise entry to Bethlehem. The Brigade Commander explained that we were going into a Palestinian city to show our presence, so the Palestinian population would understand the IDF can go wherever it wants, whenever it wants.

We went into Bethlehem in a convoy of armored IDF jeeps. We were welcomed by a barrage of stones; I really didn't understand what the meaning of this taunting was. What's the reason for entering a Palestinian city, just like that? "Sowing presence" was and remains a despised IDF practice that I got to know back during my Golani service.

One night, the Company Commander left the section for a meeting with the Battalion Commander, and I was left in charge of the company. That same night, one of the platoons set up a stakeout by the back gate of the Migdal Oz settlement. Not far from there is the Palestinian town of Beit Fajar. After a stealth movement on foot, the platoon located itself at the designated point. I commanded the stakeout from my jeep. After a few hours, the lookout identified two people approaching the back gate of Migdal Oz from Beit Fajar. The force on the stakeout, on the field, also identified them using their night-vision binoculars. The soldiers reported to me that the two figures were doing something on the ground right by the gate. The lookout reported on the radio that she identified them as carrying some sort of weapon. There was no room for doubt, these were terrorists there for an attack; this doesn't happen every day. I gave the force an order to prepare to open fire. Engagement orders allowed us to open fire on anyone who had "means and intent." *Means*, meaning weapon and *intent*, meaning attempt to attack. The force reported that it was "on," meaning it was ready to open fire and the figures were quite close. All of a sudden, the Company Commander, who'd just come back to the section and heard the radio, gave a different order. He commanded them on the radio not to open fire, but rather come out of the bushes and stop them by surprising them. I thought he was wrong, that he was endangering our soldiers' lives for no reason, but he's the commander and an order is an order. I made sure my force received the order. The force stormed the two and surprised them; they put their hands up and surrendered. I immediately arrived at the scene in my jeep. We found an improvised gun, a knife and several other detonators on them. They really were planning on performing an attack; two 15-year-old boys from Beit Fajar. We cuffed them and I took them to incarceration at the base in my jeep, until the Shin Bet would arrive to take them away. How brainwashed had they been, how impervious and hateful they had inside of them that they'd gone out and carried out such a violent act?

After I placed them in incarceration, I went to the Company Commander and gave him a hug. I thanked him for changing the order; I still do. In hindsight, I'm glad we didn't kill these boys, we've spared unnecessary bloodshed on both sides. I believe they're no longer in jail. I want to believe they've grown and learned since and I wish they'd lay down their weapons. A struggle, right as it may be, shouldn't be violent. Not towards the civilian population or soldiers.

A year later, we were once again called to serve in the Territories, this time in the Tulkarm area. I was still Deputy Company Commander.

In the briefing, the Brigade Commander explained to us that the road leading to the Avnei Hefetz settlement is open only for Jews and no Palestinians are allowed on it. This road also leads to the Palestinian village of Shufa, but the IDF blocked that path by having bulldozers raising a dirt mount there. No one asked why, we just accepted things as they were. A road just for Jews. And once again, not a word on Apartheid.

An order came in from the regional brigade one day, that we

had to chase a vehicle that had just been stolen from Israel and gone into the Territories. Ituran (the tracking company) could tell us exactly where it was. We started chasing it with three military jeeps. The radio contact from Ituran guided us to one of the villages, right to a specific house. When we got there, we saw the car in a shed, its wheels stripped off, the thieves even had time to take the doors off. We knocked on the door of the next house and an elderly woman opened up. We went inside, without asking her permission, of course; we wanted to see if anyone else was in the house, maybe even the thieves. From a quick scan, we understood she was alone. We went back to the stolen vehicle, a Nissan Tiida with a Tempo company logo on it. We were told on the radio, by the brigade, that they cannot let the tow truck in since they cannot guarantee its safety. We didn't really know what to do. The Ituran contact said he's not willing to reward the thieves by letting them have the car. We agreed and started throwing rocks at the car, breaking its windshield. We took hammers out of the jeep and started banging the car; such a strange sight. A bunch of Reserves soldiers who left their families and jobs to protect their country are at a Palestinian village near Tulkarm, in full gear, wrecking a stolen Israeli vehicle. The car was inactive a few minutes later. The doors were broken, the engine was shut and even the upholstery was torn. On the way back to the outpost, I asked a friend from my company what do our actions have to do with our country's security. He didn't reply. Neither did I.

I contemplated whether I was willing to serve in the Reserves, be part of the occupation, the daily military activity against the innocent civilian population, having nothing to do with defending my homeland and the safety of Israeli civilians. I wasn't as sure of my views back then as I am now. I still went on these two stints, though my stomach churned. There, from the point of view of a civilian who's been in uniform for only a few weeks a year, I could better see the wrongs we were inflicting as soldiers. As a more mature person, I could better understand the atrocious immorality of us even being in the Territories in the first place, and just as bad, the country's security irrationality. I also understood that there's really no meaning to any officer's "morality." **My issue isn't with the army itself, certainly not the soldiers, but with the very mission that the army and soldiers are sent to carry out by the Israeli governments, no less with the state of mind of the people who choose these governments.**

A while after my Tulkarm stint, I arrived in the same area as a civilian, to harvest olives with Palestinian farmers and serve as a human shield for them from the raging violence of the Settlers. It was the first time that I came to the Territories as a civilian. I went into that same village I had snuck into on a dark night not long before, as an officer overseeing an arrest, this time as a civilian who came to help and show solidarity with its Palestinian residents. That's when I decided that I'd never set foot in the Territories as a soldier, whatever the price may be. I understood that I was no longer willing to take part in a violent and immoral occupation. I didn't have to deal with that dilemma ever since, though it's no longer a dilemma for me. I was complete with that decision and with that internal knowledge that I wouldn't serve in the Territories anymore. My battalion wasn't called up to the Territories and we performed operational activities in the Jordan and Egypt sections.

***

In 2012 I went on a Company Commander Course as part of my three consecutive months of Reserves stint. Once the course was over, I became the commander of the company where I'd started my journey as a Company Commander.

At the end of 2014, I was in my second and last year of Physical Education certificate studies, at an academic career change program at Seminar HaKibbutzim College. I planned to spend the summer between my two college years at Almagor, helping my father pick mangoes. On the day I was supposed to go to Almagor for two months, I came to say goodbye to my beloved nephews and while I was playing with them, I got a phone call from the Battalion Commander, my commanding officer, to arrive at the base immediately, as there was an emergency recruitment for a big IDF operation in Gaza called Protective Edge[21]. I put down my little nephew and told his mom, my sister-in-law, that I had to go into the army. When she asked me 'When?' I told her, "Right now." I understood from her look that she didn't quite understand what I had just told her or perhaps refused to accept it. She raised her brows in wonderment and once again asked when I would be going to the army. I told her I'd go to my apartment, pack a bag and leave as soon as possible. She started tearing up, said it didn't make sense that I was just leaving for the army, just like that; it just doesn't make sense. "Yes," I told her. "Life here is weird, but the army called, and I have to go." I came there to say goodbye before I left to work at Almagor for two months, and wound-up saying goodbye to them because I was called up to the army. Weird.

---

21   Protective Edge was a military operation launched on July 8th, 2014, following the kidnapping and murder of three Israeli teenagers in the West Bank.

Her tears stuck in my head all the way to my apartment. I called my dad and let him know that there was a change in plans and I probably won't get a chance to come work with him during that tiring mango season. I heard the disappointment in his voice, but more than that, the concern. No one really knew what was going to happen. I didn't even know what task my battalion was assigned to.

We'd already arrived at the brigade base late that afternoon, in the Eilat mountains, and realized we were drafted to replace the regular-service battalion there, so they could go on missions in Gaza. Within 24 hours, we were already in charge of the section, and from being a Physical Education student and civilian, I found myself commanding a company of combatants who were defending the southern border of the State of Israel. I was recruited for 54 days. I only visited home once that entire time. The rest of the hours, days and weeks I was busy being a Company Commander. During my spell there, I posted on Facebook, saying: "*A time to talk and a time to be silent, a time to speak up and a time to fight. I'll shout out what I have to say. But for now, I'm proud to be part of this group of combatants that's been emergency drafted to guard the southern border of the State of Israel.*"

I think it was at that time that I more profoundly understood the foolishness of war, the irrationality of the war in Gaza: instead of finding a political solution, both sides were busy spilling blood.

I went back home after almost two months of service, mentally exhausted. Commanding a company of Reserves combatants takes a lot out of you, the hardest and most significant role I've ever had. I didn't leave my Tel Aviv apartment for two weeks; I had to get some peace and quiet.

Protective Edge (July 8th – August 26th, 2014) ended and it was quiet once again. A few months later, I received a commendation letter from the Head of the Southern Command for my role as a Company Commander during that stint.

By the way, other than many casualties and destruction – both in Israel and Gaza – nothing's changed. Everything is still the same as it was before that redundant operation. The status quo is the same, Hamas controls the Gaza Strip, the Palestinians in Gaza still live under a burdened Israeli siege and the Israeli civilians in the Gaza Envelope keep living in a sense of constant insecurity. The situation at the border remains fragile, as the next operations prove. Operation Guardian of the Walls (May 10th-21st, 2021) didn't change anything either. Many casualties and wounded, including dozens of children, devastating destruction. In this case as well, a moment after the ceasefire was declared, everything went back to being exactly as it was before that useless operation. Hamas and Israel are playing with their civilians' lives.

Reserve duty is part of my life, part of my identity. My friends from the Reserves are part of my family, regardless of their political views or place of residence. When I ran in the Meretz primaries, many of them joined the party so they could vote for me, and help me get elected. Good friends of mine, some Settlers with opinions that are opposite to mine, who loathe that party, came and volunteered on primary day; they wore the party's shirts with my name on them, gave out flyers and convinced people to vote for me. I was deeply moved by that gesture. It's something only people who've served together for so long would do for one another. A stranger won't understand it.

As I'm writing this book, in 2022, I'm still serving in the Reserves dozens of days each year. I'm proud to serve as my Reserves brigade's Operations Officer, proud to serve in a brigade that's tasked with guarding the country's borders with Egypt and Jordan. Unlike many social media celebrities these days, who can mostly write hollowed slogans about their love for the country and add empty words regarding their admiration of IDF soldiers, I also serve in the army. I don't dodge service, don't make up excuses, I wear the uniform and go out there to defend my country, even if it doesn't fit my schedule. I despise the widespread phenomenon of celebrities expressing their love for their country, who think it's important to show how patriotic they are and how much they love IDF soldiers but haven't actually served or did everything they could to serve in the combative roles. In today's Israeli society, it doesn't really matter what you did for your country. On the "scale" of good citizenship, if you're right-wing, you'll automatically be defined as "loving your country" more than someone who's left-wing, no matter if they still serve in the Reserves or are even Deputy Chief of Staff. This is the equation that was formed here. Left-wing is a derogatory term, even if you used to be the Head of the Shin Bet, and right-wing means pride, even if you were a Jewish terrorist in the past or used some kind of an excuse to drop out of military service.

During Operation Guardian of the Walls – as I've mentioned, another useless operation that claimed the lives of hundreds, among them women and children, Israelis and Palestinians – I was called for a Reserves stint at the Home Front Command, to help the Negev district deal with the many missiles dropped at the Beer Sheva area. I came right away. An hour after I arrived, a missile dropped in the Beer Sheva industrial zone. I went to the drop site with the district commander. We wanted to gauge the damage and obviously manage the required evacuation actions. The district commander immediately started isolating the area, as we got there, and worked with the rest of the civilian authorities. The police established a parameter with red tape; photography crews and curious civilians gathered beyond the tape, and I stood at the side with some of the officers from the district. Suddenly, one of the civilians recognized me from TV. He started cursing at me, screamed at me for being a traitor and that I shouldn't be in uniform and repeated the fact that I was "left-wing" quite a bit. A surreal situation. There I was, in uniform at a missile strike site and he was screaming at me that I was a hater of Israel and a traitor. I kept talking to the officers and ignored him, but he wouldn't let go, came closer to us and kept cursing me, among other things, wished me death and cursed my family as well, especially a certain occupation he suggested my mother might take on. He couldn't be ignored at some point; he was actually in our way. I didn't want to confront him, not while on duty. The officers and soldiers around me moved in discomfort; they also didn't know how to deal with the odd situation. One of the officers asked him to stop, but it didn't help. After a while, he got tired and walked away, and I was left with that experience. When I went back to the base, I acted as if nothing had happened, but I still thought of that guy. **How much incitement, lies, and hatred he had to absorb for him to stand where a missile had just struck, recognize me in my uniform and vigorously curse me? I felt sad for us as a society, not personally for him or even me.** I think this is one of the more prominent situations that showed me just how divided our people is, how much hatred towards the other is rooted in so many people, and how long a road we have to take until we can change and heal.

Chapter Six

Breaking the Silence

During one of the breaks in the first week of my academic year, I came across a stand of the *Breaking the Silence* organization. I was fresh out of my nearly two-month Reserves service, as part of "Protective Edge", and mostly carrying baggage regarding that violent and useless operation that took place in Gaza. I heard about the organization, but didn't actually know it. I talked about it with the guy at the stand, who proudly wore a black t-shirt with a prominent logo of the organization on it. After he told me a little bit about them, he asked me if I'd served in the Territories. I told him I'm a Company Commander, a Major in the Reserves who'd just returned from an emergency recruitment, but this time I didn't serve in the Territories, though I did back in 2000-2010. He asked me if I was willing to give a testimony to Breaking the Silence. I flinched at first. That kind of testimony sounded to me like treason, an action against the military. I said that I'd think about it, but I don't think I have anything to testify about since I never broke an order, I was a normative officer at Golani. He said it shouldn't be a problem and that he believes my testimony has value. After some thought, I felt I had to start doing something against the occupation and this kind of testimony is definitely a contribution to the fight. As modest of a contribution as it is, it's certainly better than nothing. I agreed to testify and we scheduled an interview. I replayed events from my service in my head in the days before the interview, both from my regular service in Golani and the two operational stints I had in the Territories in the Reserves. A few days later, the two interviewers from Breaking the Silence arrived at my apartment. They were a few years younger than me but seemed serious and professional. They introduced themselves, talked about their past as combatants in the IDF and their role in the organization's testimony and research department. The conversation was recorded for transcribing. On one hand, I felt strange in that situation, especially since I was recorded. On the other hand, for the first time in my life, I felt I was starting to do something meaningful against the occupation. After so many years of serving in the Territories, in missions I didn't believe in, here I was doing something as a civilian.

I first told about my journey in the military and then about events I thought were problematic. I talked about the violent entries into Jenin to lay endless siege on the civilian population, about the unnecessary checkpoints, the special training task on that family at Baqua ash-Sharqiyya, the Nablus operation, the abusive Magav soldiers and my relationships with the Settlers as an officer; the fact that they're actually the real commanders. I talked for three hours, almost non-stop. There were obviously no secrets or sensitive information in my testimony, just what my routine as a combatant officer in the Territories looked like. In hindsight, I understand that my testimony accentuated just how wrong our presence in the

Territories was wrong, in my view. The fact I could talk about my military service years after, about events that seemed completely normal back then and suddenly seemed terrible and morally forbidden, was very significant for me. While giving the testimony, I truly understood the importance of what Breaking the Silence is doing. Their purpose is to show the Israeli civilians what the reality looks like in the field, how much that reality is bad and has to be changed, because it cannot continue this way. I suddenly realized that I'd never even told these stories to my family and friends, and I guess it was the same for most of the people who served there. I understood how great the gap was between what I was doing there and what most Israeli citizens know and think. There's this common belief that the IDF is constantly fighting terrorists in the Territories, and that's far from the truth. The IDF spends most of its time policing, practicing absolute control over Palestinian lives. Most of my military service has little to nothing to do with the security of the State of Israel. My military service in the Territories was mainly about letting the Settlers fulfill their ideology, that this is the land of our forefathers and no matter how much Israeli or Palestinian blood will be spilled in its name. Furthermore, the Settlements damage the country's security since their positions make it impossible to draw a firm border between the Palestinians and the State of Israel, allowing terror factors to enter the country and execute terror attacks. An army can best protect the country when there's a clear border between the parties, whether that border is a result of peace or war. The Settlements created a situation in which no such border could be formed between the two people, putting the State of Israel in actual danger. Moreover, IDF soldiers' blood is spilled in vain in the name of these Settlements. Many of our soldiers wouldn't have died had they not had to aimlessly patrol between Settlements. Adding to that, the Settlements are the true, and probably the only, barrier in the way of a peace treaty between Israel and the Palestinians, which is exactly the opposite of the false narrative that's been fed here in the media and the education system for the past 20 years. We're being lied to saying the Settlements protect the rest of the country; most of the heads of the Defense System who leave their posts admit that this isn't at all the case, rather the other way around. The Settlements damage the country's security.

I felt relieved at the end of my testimony for Breaking the Silence. It was important for me to have my voice heard and this was my first platform. A few weeks later, they called me and said my testimony was approved and went on the website anonymously, as I'd requested. Why anonymously? I wasn't completely ready to be exposed yet, I feared the reaction of the people around me. I went on their website, which mostly has testimonies by soldiers like me, and looked from mine by rank and brigade. I was surprised to find out that only a small part of my testimony was published, less than a third. I called to ask them why most of my testimony was omitted and their reply was surprising. They had no doubt I was reliable and honest, but they had a protocol for testimony releases and within it they had to cross-reference it with other testimonies, media publications and other means. Since it's been quite a few years, they had trouble finding evidence for some of my stories and they'd rather not publish things they're not 100% sure are true. I was very impressed by their honest and professional work.

Two years later, in 2016, the Middle East Studies department at Ben Gurion University decided to award Breaking the Silence with the Berelson Prize. In an extreme, and anti-democratic step, the president of the university, Rivka Carmi, decided to cancel this decision claiming the organization "is controversial." These were the days of Netanyahu's absolute reign, and the bad, anti-democratic winds were starting to blow harder across the country. An alternative ceremony was held in response to the president's decision, where they awarded the organization with an alternative prize. I decided to go to that ceremony. It was important for me to show my support of the organization.

The evening began with a lecture by the late author Amos Oz, and to be perfectly honest, this was the incentive I needed to go all the way to the southern capital. Amos Oz named a list of 'traitors' from the Jewish people's history, meaning individuals – or at least some of them – who were referred to as traitors. He named, among others, the prophet Jeremiah, Herzl, Biyalik, A.B. Yehoshua and, of course, Rabin and Peres. He went on to name 'traitors' from other countries, such as Churchill, Gorbachev, Emile Zola, Abraham Lincoln and many other good people. Amos Oz declared that he was happy to be called a traitor at this time, and that Breaking the Silence should also be proud of being called that.

He was followed by the organization's then-CEO, Yuli Novak, who gave a speech that in proper times and place would be taught at each school the following day. Her words were truer, more powerful than I'd heard before. Yuli didn't talk about the soldiers' testimonies, she talked against the occupation. Yuli talked about the courage of defying consensus, about cowardly politicians, those who oppose occupation and support Breaking the Silence yet are afraid of the primaries. And I, sat there on the steps, eyes glistening with tears, feeling somewhat pride about giving my testimony to the organization two years before, for my very humble contribution to the fight against the occupation. I think it was there I understood I wanted to be part of Breaking the Silence.

Chapter Seven

From Thought to Practice

After a few years of engaging in sports and physical education, I decided to take a break. It was 2016, and I'd spent the entire year travelling Europe and working on small security projects. I mostly took time to think about what would be next in my life, as I discovered dozens of beautiful European cities. Politics, mainly fighting the occupation, started bubbling up within my body. I'd written quite a lot about the occupation on Facebook, but not much more than that. The turning point came, rather surprisingly, through sports. I was deep into endurance sports at the time: very long runs, ultra-marathons and Ironman competitions. I ran 60, 80 and 100km across five Ironman competitions, a competition that included a 3.8km swimming leg, a 180km bike riding leg and a 42km marathon to finish it all off. Four of those competitions had been in Eilat, intimate contests that felt like a small, cohesive community, with about 200 people competing in all legs. I'd gone there to compete every January since 2013. During one of the last training sessions, I thought of how to end this grueling competition. A good friend of mine from Ramallah made sure to bring me a Palestinian flag, which I attached to the Israeli flag with pins. I spent the entire competition thinking about that final moment when I'd wave the joint flags. I wanted to send a message of peace and reconciliation, I wanted for us to remember the Palestinian people living beside us even in the purest place of sports, where people push their human limits, 'and that we have to make sure we make peace with the notion, because ultimately, we're all people who wish to be free. I made sure one of the friends who came to cheer me on would give me the flag in the last kilometer. I stopped about 20 meters away from the finish line and spread out the two flags. That's how I walked all the way to the finish line as the confused announcer called out my name. Why confused? Because just like the other dozens of people in the crowd, he didn't know how to react to my gesture. Even after I crossed the finish line, I stood there for a minute and proudly waved the two flags. The following day I got a call from a well-known sports website that wished to interview me. In the published interview I explained why I'd chosen to wave both the Israeli and Palestinian flags after a 14-hour competition. Following the interview, I received an exciting e-mail from Avrum Burg, a former Member of Parliament, Chairman of the Knesset and Chairman of the Jewish Agency. In the e-mail, he wrote that he appreciated the way I'd chosen to end the race, and encouraged me in the face of any derogatory comments. I was excited to receive such an e-mail from a person I really admired, a central figure in the Israeli public. That week I realized what the right thing to do at that time in my life was: to fully engage in politics and the fight against the occupation. Thirteen years after being discharged from the IDF, and seven years since that last time I set foot in the Territories as a soldier, I decided 'to dedicate all my time to fighting the occupation; this was the right moment in my life for that.

Decisions are all well and good, but there weren't exactly politicians lining up at the entrance gate to Almagor asking to work with me. In fact, I had no contact with any politician or any political entity. Sometimes life just works out, the world has its own rhythm. A good friend of mine who worked in Kafr Qassem back then spoke about me with MP Esawi Frej of the Meretz Party. He told him about his weird friend who served in the Reserves, gave testimony to "Breaking the Silence" and had just waved both Israeli and Palestinian flags at a sports competition. Esawi was intrigued and asked to meet me. He called me and wanted to schedule a meeting. I was thrilled: a member of the Israeli Parliament had called me and gone to the trouble of clearing his schedule to meet with me. Indeed, a few days later we scheduled to meet for coffee at a Rosh HaAyin commercial center. As usual, I was early for the meeting and waited for him there. As he arrived, he immediately apologized and said he forgot he had a lecture in Jerusalem, and wondered if I wanted to join him so we could talk on the way. We connected from the very first moment. I told him about myself, and he told me about himself. After his lecture, we had a late dinner, around midnight, at an Arabic restaurant in Kafr Qassem. We couldn't stop talking, we both felt the good vibes we shared. When dessert arrived, he asked if I wanted to come work for him, to be his parliamentary consultant. I immediately agreed. Esawi was the one who opened the door for me to Israeli politics, and I'll never forget that.

***

In the first few months, I got to learn about parliamentary work at the Knesset (the Israeli Parliament). Everything was new to me: bills, queries, the work of various committees, and just getting to know this large and convoluted building called the 'Israeli Knesset'. I was at Esawi's side for most of the day, from the moment he left home until he returned there, including weekends. It was the best school for politics I could've attended. We spent a lot of time and effort nurturing relationships with various Meretz people around the country, mostly in Arab society. This led to me visiting almost every Arab settlement in Israel along with Esawi. I think this was the greatest gift I've received from my choice to peruse politics. It's a true privilege to get to know Arab society in depth, to sit in their homes, understand their culture, get to know the people and mostly understand the complexities of being an Arab in the State of Israel. I've acquired true friends all over the country, some of them have stayed in touch with me even after I left the party. But just as importantly, I further understood the huge distance between Jewish and Arab societies. I'd considered myself a Zionist back then; I came from a Zionist family, was brought up on the lap of Zionism, and that was how I saw myself, a left-wing Zionist. Zionism was a positive value for me. By talking to countless Arab/Palestinian citizens (many Arabs citizens in Israel define themselves as Palestinian), I realized 'the meaning many of them see in Zionism. No matter how I defined my own Zionism, at the end of the day many Arab citizens in the State of Israel will see it first and foremost as defining Jewish supremacy over the Arab citizens of this country. As long as I defined myself as a Zionist, I'd be drawing a clear line between myself and my fellow Arab citizens. I'm not interested in being superior to anyone, certainly not my neighbor in Galilee or Jaffa. Without getting into too much of an argument over its original intent (though I believe it was the same), Zionism today is about preserving Jewish superiority. You can see the most distinct expression of that in Zionist institutes. You can even see it on the official website of JNF', one of the most prominent Zionist entities in Israel, where it says:

"KKL-JNF was founded in 1901 and since then it has served as the operational arm of Zionism. In the name of the Jewish people, KKL-JNF bought 2.6 million dunams of land, prepared land for agriculture, founded settlements and laid the foundations for the establishment of the State of Israel... Since then, and until the second decade of the 21st century, KKL-JNF has executed thousands of projects on Israel's land. These projects include establishing hilltop villages in Galilee, buildings security roads on Israel's borders, preparing land for agriculture and for living in the Arava, the Golan and the Negev..."

Of all the projects JNF has pursued, there were zero Arab settlements. Zero. Since the JNF's foundation, it has been stripping the Arab population of lands and giving them to Jewish owners. I can certainly understand this activity prior to the establishment of the State of Israel, when the Jewish people were fighting for a country to call home, but there was no justification for this once the State of Israel was established and we were all supposed to be equal citizens – Jews and Arabs – entitled to enjoy the development of this country. JNF, by definition, is 'the operational arm of Zionism', and is at work stripping lands from Arab citizens even today while also making sure that no new – or, God forbid, existing – Arab settlements be expanded. This is the embodiment of Zionism in 2022.

I want all Israeli citizens to be equal, but to also feel that way.

The Zionism of today won't allow this for its Arab citizens – one of every five people in Israel is Arab.

When I thoroughly realized what Zionism means today and how it is perceived by many of its citizens, I understood that I no longer wished to be called a Zionist. I gave up that layer everyone so loves to flaunt around here – "Zionist". **I can love this country, be invested in its existence, and even be willing to die defending its borders without being called a Zionist. I'm an Israeli by national identity,** just as a Jewish, Muslim, or Christian person in France identifies themselves as French.

By extension, I believe the country's national symbols should represent all its citizens, and not exclude 20% of the population. I want a Supreme Court judge and the Israel National Team Captain to be able to stand up and sing the national anthem just like any other citizen, even if they're not Jewish; I certainly think it's proper to adjust the anthem so that Arab citizens can also identify with it and sing it. This is a national interest. I'll leave the task of finding the exact lyrics to wiser people than me.

I have no doubt that my main insight working with Esawi was the essential need for promoting Jewish-Arab partnerships, certainly in terms of politics. I believe, with all my heart, that the only way for a better and more proper future for Israel lies in Jewish-Arab political partnership. This is exactly what's missing in our politics. We have Meretz, which is an entirely Jewish party with a handful of Arab representatives. Cynics might say that Meretz has an Arab or two mostly so they can boast about having any Arabs at all. There's Hadash, an entirely

Arab party with Jewish representatives here and there, but one might also say they do so in order to flaunt the Jewish-Arab partnership. There's no real Jewish-Arab party, this is the vacuum on the left side of the Israeli political map.

I quickly got into Meretz's affairs, learning how a political party works in general, and this one in particular. How deeply disappointed I was! From a distance, Meretz seems like an honest, clean party, with members who only deal with promoting the party's ideologies which are so important for Israeli society. I thought Meretz was different than the other political parties, but I was wrong again. The more party members I met, the more I realized that each Member of Parliament was mostly occupied with increasing or maintaining their power within the party. When I say 'mainly occupied', I mean that most of their time is dedicated to that, with a bit given over to actually promoting ideologies and Parliament projects. Meretz is composed of several divisions that are controlled, quite literally, by politicos. The politico is sometimes the MP themselves, while at other times they make sure their representatives are their proxies, fully controlled by them.

There has been a committee at Meretz comprised of 1,000 representatives for ages. Its elections are held once every few years, according to electoral districts. This is meant to create a situation in which every part of the country has representation in the committee, relative to its population and electoral size. The committee's representatives are elected by all the people registered with the party. Registering with Meretz means paying a symbolic fee of 80 NIS per year. The point is that committee elections mainly interest the interest-holders, meaning politicians and politicos. This leads to a state in which the committee isn't comprised of ideological people who identify with the values of the party, but groups of interest-holders for promoting this or that person, and so the more committee representatives you have under your "control" – who will vote for whatever you tell them to – the more power you have in the party. When committee elections approach there's always extra effort made by politicos to get as many people to join the party as possible, so they can get many representatives into the committee who'll be loyal to them. Everyone takes part in this political game, which is completely legal but also stinks. This creates a situation in which you can find family members, close friends, and other people linked to Members of Parliament among the committee members. This is problematic, as the committee is the entity that makes all the party's decisions, including who will be the Members of Parliament on its behalf. The party's politicos have turned registering with the party into an art form, their control is down to individual members of the party, and everyone knows everyone.

I very quickly made it clear to Esawi that I wanted to go into politics so I could be one of the decision-makers, and I also started registering people and asking family members and friends to be committee members on my behalf. I was new to the game, but I played it. The elections for the Meretz committee were held at the end of 2017, and I managed to get quite a few people into it, meaning I had political power. Coupled with Esawi, we both served as a force to be reckoned with in the party.

Some of the people at Meretz didn't take kindly to my swift

(perhaps too swift) entry into party politics, and rumors started circling about me. One of the party's female MPs, who saw me as her political rival, was heard telling people I was a Shin Bet secret agent sent to make sure "Esawi was kept in line." How cruel and bigoted do you have to be in order to say something like that and start such a rumor?

I came to the party as it was changing before my eyes. In my first year there, the Chairwoman was Zehava Galon. I had the privilege of being part of the team that fought to keep her in her position. Zehava has always led a clear and persistent line of fighting the occupation and being pro-human rights. However, many politicos worked against her, mostly because she didn't take them into consideration. And they succeeded: Zehava, who had tried to open the party to new audiences and who had a hard time taking power away from the Meretz committee – meaning the politicos – had to endure a lot of venom and insults. The sentiment against her became toxic, and she wisely and gracefully decided to step aside and not run for the position again. A different Chairwoman was elected in her place, who led a distinct centralized line. She and her people thought that eyeing the center and blurring the party's real messages would strengthen it. That's when I started a forum along with other members that acted to promote Jewish-Arab political partnership within and beyond Meretz. Among other things, we demanded that all the party's publications also be in Arabic, and offered new ways to deepen Meretz's loose relationship with the Arab society in Israel in general, and especially with the Arab parties. We brought up another suggestion, for Meretz not to send representatives to Zionist institutions since they were acting to further deepen the occupation and racism. The new head of our division was startled by our actions, mostly because the chief politico of that division had a luxurious position in the Zionist Organization, with a hefty salary and plenty of time to engage in committee matters and registering people. The sense was that the party's Chairwoman was doing all she could to break up the forum, while rejecting our suggestions. As I mentioned, I demanded that the party's campaign for the first elections of 2019 include Arabic. The campaign manager plainly told me that they'd looked into it, and that any Arabic writing on the posters would lead to voter defection, so they decided to only have Arabic writing on party posters that were put up in Arab settlements.

That same politician later realized her mistake and changed her ways. The next time she ran for Chairwoman, she was leading the Jewish-Arab political line. While allegedly fashionably late, it suited her politically at the time, but I guess better late than never.

This was the Meretz I knew, a party split into divisions. There's bitter rivalry and sometimes even hatred between members of the different divisions. I felt this rivalry mostly revolved around positions and power, and very little of it was about ideology. The divisions within Meretz mostly hurt the party's functioning. The latter Chairwoman I've mentioned had the strongest division in the party acting against her, calling themselves the "Reds". The Reds are impressively run by a young man, an Organization politico whose main role is to manage a network of registered members. The network operates with the help of salaried position-holders who spend most of their days bringing in registrations, perpetuating their grip on the party and its institutions. In fact, the Reds – led by that politico – control the party completely. They made sure to crown the Chairman only if he did what that division ordered of them, mostly acting in the favor of that politico.

Parliament dispersed at the end of 2018, and for the first time Meretz went to primaries in order to elect the list of members for the next Parliament, a preliminary election by all the party's registered voters – a total of 30,000 votes. I decided to run. I knew I couldn't realistically land a spot, but it was important for me to get into the big leagues and be part of that small candidates' division that made Meretz keep waving that occupation-fighting flag. I put in my own money, and another large amount that had been fundraised. I spent almost two months on a campaign that included panels and meetings all across the country, professional videos, building a website and creating printed materials from flyers to roll-ups. Primaries are a celebration of democracy. At the end of the primaries, I reached number 14 on the list, ultimately number 15 due to gender-balancing. I was content with the result and my position. I was part of the party's lineup for the upcoming elections, and represented it on many panels.

One of those panels took place at a senior citizens' club in Haifa. When I arrived, I saw that one of the participants was Oren Hazan, a former Likud MP who was now running with his own list. We'd never met and he didn't know me, or so I thought. As the panel started, Oren practically took the microphone from the moderator and asked to say something. He pointed at me and said it was important that people know a traitor was sitting here, an Israel-hater who supported

"Breaking the Silence". I stood up and said to his face that he was a liar and inciter of hatred, all before the panel even started. As it turned out, Oren had done his homework and watched my videos, the ones I'd made for the Meretz primaries. In one of them, I spoke about the testimony I'd given to "Breaking the Silence", and the need to establish a Palestinian state alongside the State of Israel. The two-hour panel was mostly the two of us bickering. At some point there were calls coming from the audience, someone called me a "Kapo[22]". I stood up, grabbed the microphone and told them about my grandmother, who had survived Auschwitz, and my grandfather who had also survived the Holocaust and came to this country to fight in the '48 War of Independence. I told them about myself and my contribution to the country's security, and that I bet they were turning over in their graves hearing their grandson being called that. I completed my statement with a question directed at Oren: "What have you done to contribute to the country's security lately?" There was silence in the hall. Oren mainly continued his populistic slogans and incitement. At the end of the panel, quite a few people came up to me to shake my hand; it felt good. Oren tried luring me in with a low blow on the way out; as I was leaving the hall, he called out: "Shoo, go home" as if creating a situation where he was kicking me out, even though the panel was over and I had to go to another one. I was really raging at that point, and told him he was the last person who'd teach me about morals and values. Behind him was an older man who wouldn't stop shouting "traitor" and "Kapo" at me. Our conflict was captured on video

---

22   Kapo was a Jewish prisoner in a Nazi camp who was assigned by the SS guards to supervise forced labor or carry out administrative tasks regarding their fellow prisoners.

and made waves in local media. For the first but certainly not the last time, I saw how incitement looked in real-time, how false slogans can be used to incite people in a crowd. But if I have to be honest, I'd forgotten that encounter by the next morning; I didn't really care about him. How could I know that the next time I'd meet Oren would be on *Big Brother*. Life can be so surprising.

Unfortunately, Meretz's campaign for that election – and the three rounds that followed – were mostly characterized by running away from the political issue of dealing with the occupation. I couldn't vote for such a party. I started believing what people said about it, that it was a small Tel-Avivian party that mostly cared about itself. Its politicos had no ideology other than the desire for positions, just like all the other parties the political left despises. The politicos' absolute control led Meretz to the fringes of the pleasant realms of the Israeli political left. Meretz is trying to obscure its struggle against the occupation and now mostly deals with social and environmental issues. Meretz's heart and soul were rooted out, and now it's just another Zionist party with a left-wing orientation. I tried to be part of the powers that shaped it, but I was a minority even within the party's elite. The majority of Meretz preferred the positions of those closest to them over an ideology of human rights and an uncompromising fight against the occupation. Meretz has been doing more of the same, year after year. The same people, the same politicos. Meretz holds no new message for the Israeli public, certainly not for the tired and frustrated political left. But the leadership of the party has also committed what I consider to be their worst sin: They do all they can to close ranks and not let new people take hold of new positions within the party. All kinds of tricks like regulation changes and strange decisions by the party's committee (which, as you already know, is controlled by a few politicos) led them to kick out – or at least pull back – people who have a true calling within the party. There's a long list of great people who wanted to contribute to the party, but the old guard made sure to primarily preserve their own strength and make sure no one could touch their precious toy called Meretz.

When I realized I couldn't change the party, and that the control of the politicos is absolute, I decided to leave. I went into partisan politics in order to make a difference, to be part of the struggle against the occupation and for peace, and when I realized it wouldn't happen at Meretz and there was nothing I could do to change it, I had no choice but to leave.

One of the political left's main issues is their unwillingness to stare reality in the face. For quite some time now, a considerable part of the public – myself included – that believes in a democratic Israel has become a minority. The political right has rather wisely made sure, for many years now, to divide the people, Jews on one side and Arabs on the other, mostly by rendering Arab citizens irrelevant in the political game. The past twenty years have been a right-wing Israeli version of "Divide and Conquer", shifted into overdrive for the last decade. Fate has it that those who lit the spark for the re-legitimization of Arab society in Israeli politics have become the greatest inciters against it. Facing hard times in 2021, just before his temporary great fall, Binyamin Netanyahu attempted to save his own skin by creating a new and imaginary pact with the Arab Ra'am party. His failure to do so gave a stamp of approval to the political center and left parties to make that desirable move, having been scared to do so before due to their cowardice and bigotry, and establish a government with the support of an Arab party. I doubt history will remember, among other things, that Netanyahu was the one who made the forming of a coalition with Arab parties possible. Without meaning to, Netanyahu also lay the foundations for the next best thing in the political left wing.

The political left desperately needs something new, a new party. The deliverance of that camp lies in a Jewish-Arab party that will represent the opinions of many Israelis who understand that the future of the democratic State of Israel depends on a Jewish-Arab collaboration, both political and civilian. Neither Meretz nor Hadash are the ones to do so; only a new party, free of power- and position-crazed politicos, could serve as an alternative means to what the public longs to achieve: a party comprised of representatives that actually represent the public, who lead democratic ideologies, who will guide the country back to its democratic roots. **Because we have to be honest: there's no real democracy in a place where one people have martial law over another. The State of Israel isn't a democratic country, and can only be so within the '67 border.** Yet half a million Israelis who live beyond that border force Israel to run a militant dictatorship, controlling millions of Palestinians. This militant control has created a reality in which there are two populations – Jewish and Arab – who live in the same territory, the western bank of the Jordan River, yet have two different legal systems. The Jewish population is subject to Israeli law while the Arab population is subject to martial law. There's a name for ruling over two populations in the same space yet applying different legal systems: apartheid.

The political state can only be changed if something in the political flow changes. I clearly believe this 'something' is a new Jewish-Arab party that will give a voice to a very large part of Israeli society, both Jewish and Arab populations that want to promote joint life within the State of Israel while striving to achieve peace with our neighbors.

Chapter Eight

Spokesperson for
"Breaking the Silence" – So Proud!

As mentioned, I had decided to take a step back from my activity in Meretz after the first elections in 2019[23]. When I looked back on my time there – meaning most of my waking hours over those two years – I realized that most of what I'd dealt with was internal party politics, and very little time on the reason I'd entered politics in the first place: the occupation. I had a few meetings with Avner Gvaryahu, CEO of "Breaking the Silence" at the time, and expressed how much I would like to be part of the organization. I saw – and still see – in them the spearhead of the fight against the occupation, leading the pack. Like most of the public, I also mistakenly thought the organization was about the IDF's combat morals and weeding out those who disobeyed orders. Far from it: I realized that the organization routinely and mainly dealt with what martial law on a civilian population looked like from the point of view of those who had been there as soldiers.

---

23   There were four consecutive elections held in Israel, since none of the candidates were able to form a government.

The CEO offered me a role as their Knesset representative, the one who'd make sure to promote the struggle against the occupation within the Israeli Parliament, while taking advantage of my acquaintance with Parliamentary work and the various members of Parliament. I agreed. I thought the character of the role would fit me and I could help the organization where it was the weakest, at the Knesset. And there was another thing we had to agree on: my monthly wages. Unlike the lies and fake news being spread about left-wing and human rights organizations, the salaries in these civil sector companies are excruciatingly low. I asked for a reasonable sum, about the same I'd made as a Parliamentary consultant. He called me back and said that according to the organization's salary policy, he could unfortunately offer me little more than half of what I'd asked. I requested a day to think it over. I sat on my cozy balcony at Almagor and wondered about the low, almost-insulting sum of money I was being offered. I don't live a lavish life, yet my monthly expenses were significantly higher than what I was supposed to make in this case. I could work other jobs with higher wages, and live a financially comfortable life, but I came to the conclusion that in order to be part of "Breaking the Silence" – meaning to deal with the occupation on a daily basis – I'd have to scale down. I called the CEO the following day and told him that money wouldn't stop us from cooperating, and that I accepted his offer. I was at peace with my decision. I sold my car and bought a jalopy for much less; I rented a humble apartment at a moshav, thirty minutes drive from Tel Aviv, and started working for "Breaking the Silence". My overdraft at the bank would rise, but I knew I'd manage. There was such a gap between the false propaganda regarding enormous wages funded by external factors and the reality of the situation. Working for human rights organizations is almost volunteer work, and that's the truth.

As fate would have it, their spokesperson announced he was leaving the same week I started working there. The CEO then told me that what he needed, more than a Knesset representative, was a spokesperson – and asked me to fill the position. Though spokesmanship is a profession and I'd never filled such a role, I agreed to his request mostly because it was important for me that the organization succeed, and I was willing to accept any role that would contribute to what I believed to be one of the most important organizations in Israel. My friends told me I was making a mistake, that being this organization's spokesperson would forever mark me in Israeli society. "That's right," I replied, "I'm at peace with that permanent mark." I felt proud to be their spokesperson, but more than that, I felt a sense of calling. I reverently walked into their offices. During one of my conversations with the people of "Breaking the Silence", I realized that almost the entire executive level of the organization were people the IDF made sure to dismiss or simply stopped calling for Reserves service, and they expected this would be my fate as well. I was so at peace with my decision to work for the organization that I wasn't even bothered by that. I took it into account, despite it being irrational.

A few weeks after I started working there, I was called up for three weeks of Reserves service, for operational activity on the Egyptian border. Halfway through the activity, a message was released in the media that I was being appointed spokesperson for "Breaking the Silence". I could feel the murmuring and talk in the battalion, especially from the soldiers who didn't personally know me. The company commanders, just like the Battalion Commander and the rest of the staff officers, knew me well and didn't really think much about it. But there were a few soldiers who came up to me and asked how I could be a spokesperson for an organization of traitors and Israel-haters, one that sought to put IDF soldiers on trial. On the one hand, I knew they were speaking out of ignorance, but on the other hand, these soldiers mirrored the atmosphere in Israeli society towards "Breaking the Silence". Years of ongoing incitement had done its job. I was ready for it, but I don't think I realized how little knowledge there was regarding the organization. The public was subject to brainwashing from right-wing Israeli politics. Far-fetched organizations were looking to besmirch human rights organizations, but the spotlight was mainly pointed at "Breaking the Silence". The reason for that hinges on the understanding right-wing people have that the activity of "Breaking the Silence" might actually succeed and damage their agenda of promoting and deepening the ongoing occupation. After all, "Breaking the Silence" is an organization comprised of ex-IDF soldiers who served, risked their lives – in the Territories among other places – and now they wanted to talk about their service; not about irregular events of abuse, but mostly the routine in the Territories, what Israeli control of the Palestinian population looks like from the viewpoint of the spearhead, those who were there. Those groups on the right realized that the Israeli people might listen to those ex-soldiers (and even current soldiers like me), who say out loud that the IDF's presence in the Territories endangers the country, endangers the soldiers and is also very bad for the Palestinians; and if you can't really argue with 1,200 soldiers testifying as to their service, what can you do? Call them all liars. Make people think they're undermining the State of Israel, incite people against them with lies, eliminate the very discussion, the argument. After all, there's no point arguing or listening to traitors and liars. Years of attempts to soil their name had penetrated people's hearts, turning the most patriotic members of society into traitors. A well-oiled incitement machine, with a lot of money and media know-how, acted and continues to act against anyone who dares go against Israel's presence in the Territories. I encountered this for the first time during my Reserves service, during operational activity, while in uniform, with a Major's rank insignia on my shoulders.

The Battalion Commander feared internal unrest during the operational activity. A few soldiers approached me in the mess hall and politely and respectfully asked to talk to me. I obviously agreed, but on one condition: no politics. This is a habit I'd had since my days as Company Commander: we don't talk politics when we're in uniform. Once we're done with the Reserves and want to meet for a coffee or a beer, we can talk about anything.

I didn't want anyone to think I was pushing my political agenda while in service. I think this is wrong, and a terrible thing to do. I finished my meal and went out to talk to the soldiers over coffee. A group of about ten men I didn't know, combatants from one of the companies, gathered around me. They asked all the right questions, mostly wanting to know why I'd decided to be a part of "Breaking the Silence". I replied in the most honest way possible: I told them what the organization actually did, what their real activity is. At one point one of the soldiers said he thought something else entirely, and now that I'd explained it to him – though he still didn't agree with it – he understood its legitimacy. **I realized the gap that lay between what the Israeli public thought and knew about "Breaking the Silence", and the reality.** It seems that was also when the first seeds were planted for me to join *Big Brother*. We hugged it out and each went on their military routine.

Later during that stint, I received a phone call from the organization's CEO. He wanted me to find the time to get to our offices, since there was an urgent matter he wanted me to join in my capacity as a spokesperson. Two days later I found some time and drove for three hours to Tel Aviv to meet him. I walked into the offices at noon, in uniform and with my rifle, since I'd come straight from my Reserves stint and had to go back as soon as the meeting was over. We talked for two hours, made some decisions regarding the matter, and then I went back to the army. It turns out my arrival at the offices in uniform stirred some mixed feelings among some of the employees. Even though they knew about my Reserves service, a few of them still had a hard time seeing me in uniform like that. I don't know if anyone had ever walked into their offices in uniform before, but to me it was natural, part of my world. Even though most of them are ex-soldiers, some employees see the IDF as an occupation army and nothing else, though they are the minority and certainly don't represent the organization's point of view.

When I returned to the organization from my Reserves service, I was asked what the reactions there had been and whether I'd been thrown out. I told them about the mixed feelings, the conversations, and replied that I hadn't been kicked out at all. On the contrary, a few days after it was over, I got a call from the Brigade's Chief of Staff, who wanted to offer me the position of Operations Officer, a senior and very important role. I told him I was willing to take on the challenge, but that it was important for me to be honest with him and the Brigade Commander about my civilian job. I told him my Reserves service obviously had nothing to do with my work, but I still wanted them to acknowledge it. He replied that he'd pass the information along to the Brigade Commander and that they'd make a decision. A few days later, I was summoned to a meeting with the recently-instated Brigade Commander. We had a pleasant introductory meeting, and among other things I told him who I was and what I was doing. Surprisingly, he wasn't too bothered by it, and directly – and quite bravely, if I might add – told me that as he saw it, "Breaking the Silence" is a legitimate organization in the country, and regardless of his own opinions, he saw no issue with promoting me to the position of Operations Officer. He also added that he'd received excellent recommendations about my performance as an officer in the Reserves, and would love to appoint me to the role. We shook hands and said goodbye, agreeing on my new position in the Reserves. The following day, I told my friends at "Breaking the Silence" about the Brigade Commander's decision to appoint me to the role, and they were all amazed.

Let's be clear, there are many opinions in the organization, and there were also people in the organization who criticized me for still serving in the Reserves. But just as I was at peace and proud of my work with "Breaking the Silence", so too was I at peace and proud of my Reserves service, certainly service within the peaceful borders we share with Egypt and Jordan for the past ten years, along with the operational challenges and unique dangers these sectors possess.

Later, that same Brigade Commander would have to answer to the Chief of General Staff about my appointment, due to a petition submitted to the latter demanding my dismissal from the Reserves due to my job as spokesperson for "Breaking the Silence" (and, God forbid, holding left-wing opinions). The bureau of the Chief of General Staff sent those wretched and despicable petitioners packing. The reply letter to this unimaginable request said that *"First and foremost, we should emphasize that the political views of IDF soldiers and commanders are irrelevant and do not affect their promotion or assignment to certain positions. It should be emphasized that, throughout his regular military service, Major (Ret.) Nir Cohen has performed his tasks in the most professional and concise manner, and he is appreciated by both his soldiers and commanders. Prior to Nir's assignment to this role, he vowed to keep performing his tasks in the same manner, regardless of his personal views and while separating his military role from the one he holds at 'Breaking the Silence'."*

Everything is well-known in the world of social media. All my soldiers knew my political opinions well, as did the settlers, including the radical ones. It never stopped us from serving together, nor them from serving under my command.

As Company Commander, one of my officers invited me to his newborn son's *bris*. I loved that officer like a brother, we appreciated each other both in the military as well as socially. I knew it was important for him that I attend the *bris*. The only problem was that he lived in a settlement, and I have a principle about visiting settlements. I deliberated greatly. On the one hand was my friendship and companionship with this great officer of mine, and on the other was my political views and their daily derivatives. I decided to show up. For a few moments, my value of friendship with this officer – a true friend – surpassed my political values as a citizen.

One day I happened to meet a friend of mine with whom I used to work as an Airline Marshall. Back then we were on good terms, and even once went on vacation together. I'd gone on my way and he'd stayed in the field of Security, and is currently part of a SWAT team. When I told him what I now do for a living, his face warped. He told me he couldn't understand how I became that way and simply walked away, muttering some juicy curse word at me. I once again realized the terrible label "Breaking the Silence" had been given, and how effective the propaganda machine was.

***

Public Relations was new to me, and I had to learn and expand that field. Luckily my manager was Achiya Schatz, a man with a lot of experience and knowledge in media. I learned a lot from him. As the spokesperson for "Breaking the Silence", I was entrusted with keeping in touch with journalists and various TV editors. Part of the media work required us to make appearances, give interviews and publish columns in newspapers and websites. After the years of pummeling the organization had suffered, this was a hard task. Yes, *Haaretz* published almost anything I asked of them, but other newspapers and TV channels were a lot more challenging. They usually asked us to comment on events that took place in the Territories. One of those times, we wanted to publish an opinion essay on one of the biggest and most widespread news websites in Israel. I called the editor of the Opinions section and introduced myself. I sent him the essay and waited for his reply. I tried getting hold of him for about 10 days, and he simply avoided me. Finally, he replied that they weren't interested in letting "Breaking the Silence" be heard, and that he wouldn't publish the essay. I once again felt frustrated due to the lack of fairness directed at us. Reality had narrowed down the organization's presence to places where they're already preaching to the choir, such as *Haaretz* and similar entities. I felt we weren't reaching new audiences, "we" being not only "Breaking the Silence" but the entire anti-occupation camp. We were limited to a small and very specific field, and there was no way we'd get more sympathy that way. So yes, it's nice to be appreciated by certain authors, actors, other artists and members of the cultural elite, but there'd be no chance of change if this remained our only audience. I felt this camp had been doing more of the same for a very long time, with no creative thinking, no real desire to change. We had to do some soul-searching, one that would lead us to other places, other ways. More than anything, I was worried about losing the younger generation, those who'd been born in the late 1990s and early 2000s, who mainly knew Netanyahu as Prime Minister, and moreover the faulty government culture he had spread. The average age at left-wing protests is in the 60s. The same goes for the various organizations' tours of the Territories. What we're offering isn't appealing to younger generations, people in their twenties. If we didn't realize that, we'd keep failing our mission, as we had for so many years. That was the truth. I admired the people who worked for "Breaking the Silence", for meager pay, but unfortunately this organization hadn't had any effect on new audiences in a long time. The best-case scenario was that it would manage to maintain a rather limited audience and mostly evoke antagonism in most of the Israeli public. **In spite of that, I have no doubt that history books will also mark "Breaking the Silence" as the most prominent Israeli organization to help end the occupation.** The founders of this organization, Yehuda Shaul and his friends, deserve a lot of respect from fellow peace advocates and human rights activists, and no less from people who love the State of Israel, want what's best for it and worry for its future as a democratic state.

Chapter Nine

Are We Finally Awake?

Compared to all other left-wing protests, the Balfour[24] Protest of 2020 was different. There were two substantial things that made it so: first, the protesters' age. It was the first time since the Social Protest that I'd seen so many young people take to the streets, one Saturday after another, for months on end, just to protest the situation. The second was the fact that the issue of occupation wasn't hidden or blurred out. When the social protest of 2011 broke out, its leaders made a terrible decision not to link the high cost of living with the fact that Israel had invested billions of shekels into developing and maintaining the Settlements in the Territories. That decision stemmed from the desire to bring as many people to the streets as possible. Their operation was successful, yet the patient still died. They managed to get many citizens to protest, but it failed and died out. Since 2011, the cost of living in Israel has just kept rising. I refused to take part in that social protest as I thought it was impossible to talk about the distress of Israeli citizens without mentioning one of its main causes. Furthermore, it made no

---

24   Balfour Street, Jerusalem, the location of the Israeli Prime Minister's residence.

sense to me that people were shouting for social solidarity in the streets, yet forgot or ignored the millions of Palestinians under martial law just a 30-minute drive from Tel Aviv. Years later I had the honor of sitting through an entire evening with Daphni Leef, the leader of that social protest, and discussing with her what I thought of that protest. You should ask her if she was convinced. Stav Shafir and Itzik Shmuli, who managed to leverage the success of the social protest into political power, later became Members of Parliament who didn't deal with the Israeli-Palestinian conflict at all. There's a reason the left wing pushed them out; there are enough centrist people in Israel. During my time as the spokesperson for "Breaking the Silence", there was an upheaval against then-Minister of Education Rafi Peretz, who supported conversion therapy. A protest was held at the plaza in front of the government offices in Tel Aviv, and some "Breaking the Silence" employees also arrived with a huge poster that denounced the minister's statements. At the bottom of the banner was the organization's logo, and we wore shirts with the organization's logo while holding the big sign. I noticed one of the Labor Party's MPs also arriving at the protest at one point; she noticed the sign, came up to us, and the second she noticed the "Breaking the Silence" logo she quickly moved over to the other side of the demonstration, so that God forbid she not be affiliated with us. I remember thinking this was one of the side effects, the result of the propaganda machine that's been working against human rights organizations these past few years – MPs on the center and left of the political map are actually afraid to be seen with us, so they won't be besmirched for supporting those kinds of organizations. Even though there is no direct link, I admit I was pleased that Shafir and Shmuli weren't reelected to Parliament, since I hoped other MPs from the Labor Party would be elected who didn't think it was right to ignore the occupation, and were proud to support human rights organizations.

The Balfour Protest, on the other hand, didn't hide the link between the corruption of power and the occupation. I found myself walking the streets of Jerusalem with thousands of people around me, one Saturday after another, people of all ages but mostly the young, shouting "Stop the Occupation!" alongside calls against the corrupt in power and the then-Prime Minister.

One of the most moving marches started in the Arabic neighborhood of Silwan in East Jerusalem, and was organized by "Peace Now" and Palestinian activists from that neighborhood. At the starting point, we gathered thousands of Israelis and Palestinians and marched towards Balfour, all the while shouting against both the corrupt in power and the occupation. During the demonstration, right on the border between East and West Jerusalem, a young woman was marching next to me holding a small cardboard sign with the Palestinian flag on it. A policeman suddenly ambushed her and violently took the flag away. He claimed, falsely if I may add, that she could not wave the Palestinian flag in public. There is no law in Israel stating that the Palestinian flag cannot be waved. I couldn't control myself and demanded the policeman return that small and measly cardboard flag. I fought with them for the democratic principle of freedom of speech. No policeman will decide on their own and prevent legal presentations of the Palestinian flag. The march was stopped and people gathered around me and the policemen; things got heated. The policemen agreed to return the flag only if the woman promised not to wave it. How symbolic, right on the border between democratic Israel and occupying Israel, a policeman had violently grabbed a little cardboard peace flag from a young woman. For the sake of the march, we gave up and kept on, but the powerful sense of thousands of Israelis and Palestinians marching together couldn't be wiped out. If only we knew and could have gotten together a few more joint-cause protestors, we might have been a raging river.

We thought the protest could really change the political system in Israel, especially on the left side of the political map; that the protest would pump fresh blood into politics, bring new and young people into the Israeli parliament; that those who were so full of themselves would go home and be replaced by people who had true vision and plans of action. There was a sense that the thousands of people who took to the streets for so long didn't just want to replace Netanyahu, but also shake up the entire system and bring in a new agenda.

I held onto the opinion that it was wise to translate the Balfour Protest into a new political force and create a new party from that great public outcry. I was one of the people who started a new party, called the Democratic Party, and tried to create a new partisan platform to bring the protest to Parliament. This attempt unfortunately failed, for many reasons. Financially we were low on resources and quite a few of the politically-inexperienced people in the group were the ones to set the tone. But I'm not sorry for this attempt, I'll forever prefer to be one of those who tried, even if they eventually failed, than one who only talks while fear of failure causes them to refrain from acting.

I still believe the moment will come and the political order in Israel will change. And if establishing the Democratic Party serves as an inspiration, then while this specific attempt failed in the short run, the idea of it will succeed in the long run.

Chapter Ten

Big Brother – The Campfire

My phone rang in the middle of a workday, while I was at the offices of "Breaking the Silence". The screen showed it was "Dolev from *Amazing Race*", which was how I'd saved her contact on my phone after we'd worked together on the show's production. I was surprised by that unexpected call, but after a few hollow pleasantries, she told me the real reason she'd called. She'd been trying to get ahold of Achiya Schatz, my manager at "Breaking the Silence", for a few days. She was casting participants for *Big Brother* and thought he'd be a great cast member, and could represent the organization in a way that would be good for it. Dolev asked for my help in reaching him, so that he'd at least be willing to talk to her. I obviously agreed to help.

Achiya and I had a special relationship. On the one hand he was my boss, but on the other we were also great friends. I appreciated him immensely, learned a lot about the media from him and cared about his opinion. When I told him about my conversation with Dolev, he said they'd been trying to cast him almost every season, and that they'd also tried casting other people from the organization; he refused to cooperate with them. Later that day, I told Dolev about my conversation with Achiya. She said they'd been looking for someone with a left-wing agenda to represent that side. Dolev asked for my help, and I sent out a WhatsApp message on a group chat for all the spokespeople of the left-wing organizations in Israel. I wrote about the *Big Brother* casting and asked if anyone was interested, or knew anyone who'd be good for it. There are a lot of spokespeople in this group, but none of them bothered replying. That was when it hit me. I went home and thought: *How is it possible that the casting department of Big Brother can have such a hard time finding a person who takes pride in their left-wing views, and wants to talk about them on primetime?* By the way, I'd never watched *Big Brother,* it had always seemed like trash to me and a terrible waste of time. I went on with my weekly routine as the organization's spokesperson. About a week later, Dolev called again. She asked about me, and whether I might be willing to do the show. I was surprised. I admit I hadn't even thought about it until then. I was just starting out at the organization, had been in that position for less than a year, and felt there was a lot more I could contribute before spreading out in other directions. Dolev suggested that I meet her for coffee; it was a slow day, so I agreed. Our meeting was conditional upon nothing being filmed, just the two of us talking, at my insistence. I arrived at her office within an hour, the *Big Brother* production company offices to be exact.

We had a great conversation. Dolev told me about the show's format, and I told her about my life. There had just been an exhibit by artist Quique Kierszenbaum, supported by "Breaking the Silence", that showed 52 portraits of soldiers who'd broken their silence alongside testimonies from their military service, against 52 years of occupation – a big and expensive project I'd helped lead. I took pride in that exhibit, and the fact that my picture was also in it. As we were talking, her boss came in and started to pseudo-interview me. After a few minutes, she asked if I'd be willing to meet Roy, the show's chief editor. She asked to videotape the conversation. Despite what I had agreed to with Dolev, I consented. To this day I still have no idea why. The conversation with Roy took about an hour; I mostly talked about myself and my path in life. At the end of the videotaped conversation, Roy asked if he could talk to me in his office. He said he'd love it if I participated in the show, and wanted me to agree. I on the other hand had some reservations. I knew that first of all I had to think about what I wanted to do, but I also had to talk to Achiya and the CEO of "Breaking the Silence", who had actually brought me into the organization. I felt committed to both of them as well as to the organization, and I didn't want to do anything without their blessing. I told Roy I'd think about it and that we'd talk in a few days. One thing stood out from my conversation with him: I felt his honesty and kindness. My gut feeling was right about him. I felt he was a trustworthy man who wasn't out to hurt me. This all happened about a month before the show went on the air. In terms of casting, it was well past due. Roy had to get an answer and didn't hide his urgency or stress.

The following day, as I was visiting Quique's exhibit, Dolev suddenly showed up. She'd come with a friend and was curious about the show. She was impressed by it, and in the phone conversation we had later she said she'd learned a lot thanks to it, both about the occupation and about "Breaking the Silence". I don't know if she'd come there as part of the attempt to try and convince me to go on the show, or whether she had actually been curious, but in any case, it was a sign for me that the show would allow me to talk about the occupation, about "Breaking the Silence" and the rest of the human rights organizations in a broad yet direct way, to the entire Israeli people.

The next few days were sleepless, and my head was bursting with thoughts. I tried thinking about the pros and cons, taking everything into account. I talked to Achiya and surprisingly he didn't rule it out, but asked me to think about it. Unnerved, I went to CEO Avner's office – a man who eventually became a friend, a partner on the road I was taking, and mostly someone I respected. It was evening, and only the two of us were there. As always, he just listened at first. I, on the other hand, presented him with the option to contemplate participation, though I can now say I was already inclined to accept Roy's offer. In the end he was very unambiguous, and unambiguously negative. "Breaking the Silence" has suffered terrible attacks from TV channels in recent years, including a false and despicable story on Channel 12 that presented the organization in a very negative light. The organization was experiencing relative calm during my time there, maybe because the media had dealt with it too much in prior years. The CEO was happy with the relative peace from the media, and feared that my entering *Big Brother* would damage the organization; this was mostly because what sets the tone of the show is the editing, and as mentioned, the organization had been burnt by tendentious editing. The conversation ended with the understanding that he was against it, and that I should drop it. Achiya also aligned with the CEO and voiced his objection. The two people I admired most in the organization, the ones who had become my friends but were also my bosses, completely objected to the step I was about to take. Now I was even more confused. It was a hard enough decision to go on the most-watched reality TV show, and now there was also this conclusive objection by "Breaking the Silence". I received a message from Roy, the show's editor, on my way home. He asked whether I'd already made a decision, and I replied that I needed a few more days.

There was another person whose advice I wanted to get, a media consultant who guided the organization. She was a well-known figure in the political left who had a lot of experience in media and politics. In those days she was working as the organization's external consultant, and we had a good relationship. I asked to meet her urgently, but not at the office. I told her I had to get her opinion on something urgently and discretely. About an hour after I sent the message, we were already meeting for coffee. I asked to talk to her not as an external consultant but as a friend. I told her the entire story: the offer, the objections from the CEO and Achiya, and my dilemma. I was sure she'd support my bosses' opinion; I was wrong. After talking for a few minutes, she looked at me and said: "Nir, you'll never forgive yourself or 'Breaking the Silence' if you miss this opportunity." Boom. She also added that if anyone could successfully convey the message on that show, she thought it would be me.

The meeting with the media consultant was significant for me, and after that, I decided to go with my gut feeling, no matter the cost. I knew I was taking a huge risk, but felt it was the right thing to do. Time was pressing; the show was about to go on the air in three weeks, and there was still a process to complete with production – physical exams, psychological evaluations, signing the contract, photoshoots in the days before entering the house, and of course my own personal preparations. The following day I spoke to the CEO of "Breaking the Silence" and informed him that I'd be going on the show. Avner was very disappointed, hurt and even angry. But he's an honorable person, and that was how he treated me, with respect. He asked that I not go as the organization's representative, and to make sure I clarified that. I realized he meant that going on the show would get me fired; I completely understood his demand, and accepted it. We agreed that I was done with the organization. For now. We both left the door open for me to return. I told him that as I saw things, I'd be evicted from the house within two weeks tops, since staying in the house depends on the viewers' votes, and what were the chances that Israeli viewers would keep a former spokesperson of "Breaking the Silence" on the show?

"I'll be back in two weeks, if you'll have me," I told him.

Avner said something I thought was farfetched: "What if you stay there for three months?" I snickered and said it would never happen, and that he shouldn't speak nonsense.

A few days before I went on the show, the CEO gathered the staff and informed them of my decision, in my presence. I added a few words about why I was doing it, and mostly talked about the importance of us being on primetime, not to be ashamed but proud. As I expected, most of the employees were shocked by the fact that I was going on that garbage show. Some of them were even angry and took personal offense. One of the veteran employees told me she'd spoken to someone who used to work on the show, and he'd told her it was a trap for me and that I had nothing to gain from it. It's not easy facing objections from so many people, some of whom I very much respected.

After that talk, I gathered my belongings and said goodbye to the people there. My mood was very fragile.

On the train to my temporary home in Beit Hananiya, I received a phone call from Miki Kratsman. Other than being an academic and one of the best and most highly regarded photographers in Israel, Miki was also Chairman of the Board of "Breaking the Silence", and one of the organization's founders. I'd first met Miki a few months earlier, at a seminar in South Africa teaching the region's past and present, obviously while focusing on the Apartheid era. We were a group of Israelis and Palestinians at a magical retreat, about an hour's drive from Cape Town. The schedule was hectic and we studied from dawn to dusk. Both of us, Miki and I, would wake up early and go on our exercise routine – he'd walk and I'd run. We'd see each other every morning, exchange a few words and leave for the amazing nature surrounding the farm where we were staying. At breakfast, we'd summarize our sporting activities. In the evenings, the unique South African wine helped us soften the atmosphere, and we'd talk about everything for hours. Miki is a wise and pleasant conversationalist. The age gap between us was non-existent, maybe because Miki is young at heart. We bonded at that seminar and had mutual respect for one another. During that phone call, while sitting in that train car, Miki told me he'd just heard of my decision. He added that he was against it, but if he had to choose anyone to represent him on that show, it would be me.

"Nir, we started this organization with our own two hands, it's part of my life's work," he said. "I only ask one thing of you: keep us safe. There's a lot riding on you."

That was when the tears started rolling down my cheeks. The strain and tension overwhelmed me, and Miki's words penetrated my soul. The magnitude of the task became clearer. I thanked him for the heartfelt phone call. I put an Israeli song about making the right choice on the headphones and simply started to cry. I cried as if I were alone in the dark and not in a train car full of passengers. I didn't know whether I was making the right decision.

I had a surprise waiting for me on the first day of shooting, just before entering the *Big Brother* house. Roy, the *Big Brother*, suggested – while shooting, of course – that I enter the house on a "secret mission" and play a religious settler for a few days, without the other tenants knowing my true identity, and that I keep everyone from suspecting me. Accomplishing the mission would guarantee me immunity from eviction in the first week, giving me more time in the house. I refused. I knew I could act that role out, I could accomplish that mission, but my mind wandered in a negative direction. I was afraid everyone would say that it was exactly what I was doing in "Breaking the Silence", acting and lying. At the end of the shooting day, Roy pressured me to take it on. I told him there was only one person I'd listen to, and she was the reason I took this offer in the first place; the media consultant. He asked to talk to her, but I refused. I met with her the following day and told her about the offer, that I had turned it down. First, she very wisely said: "That's the greatest gift you could've gotten. You have to accept."

Boy was she right. I let Roy know that I'd be accepting the secret mission challenge, and would enter the house as a religious settler. A few days later I reshot the footage, this time taking on the mission. As per my agreement with the organization's CEO, I said on camera that I no longer worked for "Breaking the Silence" and that I was entering the house as Nir, representing only myself. I made sure with Roy that this sentence would make it to the first segment of the show, where I introduced myself. Roy kept his promise.

A few days before the show began, I went shopping with Roy and Yoav, childhood friends of mine. Yoav had just arrived for a home visit from the U.S., where he'd been living for the past 15 years. We walked around the mall in Tiberias, going from one clothing store to another. "You understand, Cohen, that in a few weeks you won't be able to walk around here anymore? People are going to be so mad at you and hate you that they simply won't let you into their stores." I replied that I was certainly considering it as an option, and not ruling out that I might have to go to San Francisco in a few weeks until things relating to me cooled down in Israel. That was how much I feared the maneuver.

A day before I entered the house, I went to say goodbye to my beloved parents. As I was leaving, my mother started to cry. I looked at her and wondered: "What's there to cry about, Mom? In a couple of weeks I'll be right back here with you." I really believed I was going on an intense yet short adventure. Just before I got into my car, my mother asked me for one thing: "You should shave, Nir. Make it respectable."

I'd grown my beard long because of the secret mission, so I'd look authentically religious. My mother obviously didn't know about that. On my last run with my brother Yuval, I told him that failure for me would be getting evicted after one week, and success would be staying there for a month. I never dreamt of a minute longer.

I felt like I was going on a Reserves stint, this time not in uniform but dressed as a 'leftist'. In my head, I prepared for it the same as an operation, a battle.

On Monday, December 30th, 2019, at 3 PM, a taxi arrived and picked me up. I left everything behind, even my cellphone. I asked my cousin to publish a post on my Facebook page the evening I went into the house, and that was it. I didn't want to get anyone from my environment involved in this plan. In that post I wrote the following:

Why? Because it's an opportunity to talk about the occupation, human rights, equality and the Palestinians in front of the entire country. So the people of Israel will see that the 'leftist' is someone who loves his country, and that the reason I'm fighting to stop the occupation comes from a desire for both Israelis and Palestinians to have a better reality. I went into Big Brother in the name of the values guiding me for quite a few years now, and which I want to represent. The same drive that led me to serve in the military for the past 20 years, the same that led me into politics and made me break my silence – the love of this land and the people in it, Israelis and Palestinians alike.

I'd like to thank the amazing people at "Breaking the Silence" for my wonderful time with them, the right to work alongside them and the pride of breaking my silence.

One last thing, I apologize to my many good friends for not being able to update them and share this whole Big Brother thing with them. I truly couldn't, for obvious reasons.

Love you, see you on the other side

And so the adventure began.

***

The first few days in the house were very strange. I played the role of the religious settler for three days, and quite successfully too. No one suspected me. As a religious guy, I was beloved and accepted by all the tenants. I accomplished the mission and won immunity. My confession time – exposing the fact that I wasn't actually a settler but a former spokesperson for "Breaking the Silence" – was interesting. Everyone in the house was shocked, since they had actually believed me.

I could finally be myself. One of the participants, who would later become a good and close friend of mine, started cursing me. Later, in an emotionally-charged one-on-one meeting I had with one of the tenants, he claimed that people with my political views should die. I feared that sentence, since it was actual incitement. Later that day, one of the editors promised me that the line wouldn't be aired, and it wasn't.

Most of the tenants embraced me and remained friendly even after they realized who I really was. One of the most prominent figures in the show was Lior Duek. Lior and I connected from the very first moment. Once I revealed my true character, Lior made sure I knew that we were still friends. I have no doubt other tenants in the house looked up to him and did the same. The initial message was conveyed: what mattered was how a person acted and not their political opinions, a message I believe is important, especially in today's Israel. The gift that wise media consultant had talked about proved itself true. I quietly thanked her for the good advice.

Each day felt like a month. Three days in the *Big Brother* house felt like a lifetime. Sensations and emotions became even more extreme in there. After four days, they made a live announcement that another tenant would be joining us. During the commercial break, we tried to guess who it would be. I naively didn't think it would have anything to do with me. Boy, was I wrong. Toward the end of the commercial break, I noticed that all the cameras were pointed at me; there were about six or seven of them that had changed their position to face me. I told Ruth, a good friend of mine, that the tenant about to enter the house had something to do with me. My guts churned. A few minutes later, ex-MP Oren Hazan came down those steps, the man who symbolized the worst in Israeli politics and was responsible for quite a few lies and filth thrown at human rights organizations in Israel. I recalled our previous encounter at the Haifa senior center elections panel, the harsh verbal conflict and calls of "Kapo" by his supporters. Oren had been silent while those profanities were being thrown in my face; I hadn't forgiven him for that terrible moment.

Oren was warmly embraced by all the tenants, including Ruth who rose to greet him. I remained seated on that couch for a few moments. I didn't have a lot of time to think, I had to make a decision, almost on instinct. I got up and reached my hand out, thinking that I would be willing to have a dialogue even with my greatest enemy. Oren said he wouldn't shake my hand. That's when I realized I'd made the right move. The energy in the house erupted into turmoil. Duek yelled at Oren, and the rest of the tenants joined in on the criticism. I felt like I was watching a movie, and it was close, only real: a movie the entire country was watching, in which I played one of the lead roles.

For the following hour, all I could think of was they were right. Everyone who had told me not to go on that show was right, mostly the people at "Breaking the Silence". I felt defeated, confused. I went to talk to Roy, *Big Brother*, feeling that he had tricked me. I thought I couldn't be on the same platform as Oren. I told him I wanted out, that I had had enough. I activated the "24 procedure" in my contract, notifying them that I was leaving the show and they had 24 hours to convince me to stay, and if they couldn't, they had to open the house door and let me out.

As part of their persuasion, I was told that Oren had only entered the house for one week. I went out of that room and informed the rest of the tenants of my decision, with tears in my eyes. I didn't expect the intensity of their reactions. I was pressured by all the tenants to stay. They said wise words and opened my eyes. I sat down with Lior, who talked sense into me. Lior is smart and quite sagacious, what he told me made me very emotional and caused me to tear up. After talking to him, I decided to stay, come what may, but I was still very angry at the show's producers.

That week with Oren went as well as it could have for me. I felt that I was rising to battle every day, and every night I recapped what had happened that day, reviewing the battle. In hindsight, it was only once the show was over and I watched these episodes that I realized how much having him there had contributed to the message I wanted to convey. Looking back, I know I was wrong to be mad at the show's producers.

The dialogue around me was initially all about my political opinions. I had a need to say what I felt; it is why I'd entered the most famous house in the country.

The first month was very good for me. As I watched the episodes, I saw there was a lot of screentime given to me and the opinions of the anti-occupation section; my greatest victories were primetime exposure for quite a few minutes when talking about the occupied Territories and debating "Breaking the Silence" at length. I tried to make the least number of mistakes while on the show, to show my better side and not give my political enemies any ammunition. I was told that in the months I'd spent in *Big Brother*'s house, the number of people accessing the "Breaking the Silence" website had catapulted by thousands of percentages compared to previous months. That meant quite a few people were actually interested in the organization, had checked it out and tried to understand whether the propaganda was true or not. I woke up every morning with the knowledge that my days on the show were numbered, and tried to make the best of the time I had been given. During one of those times, it was decided that the voting ceremony – that same weekly ceremony secretly held in the *Big Brother* room – would be public. Many of the tenants chose to evict me due to my political opinions. Most of them said they loved me as a person, but that my political opinions were unacceptable and they wanted me out. I was glad they'd said it in public, one after the other. Their public choice was exactly the message I wanted to convey. **Without being aware of it, they were an exact mirror of Israeli society, one that**

pushes people aside just because of their opinions. I went into the *Big Brother* room and talked about it. In their miserable decision, these tenants had given me a gift. I only found out months later that a few schools had held discussions on the question of whether it was alright to evict someone from *Big Brother* due to their political opinions. Another small victory. I had started a discussion; that was why I'd gone on this show in the first place.

I formed a routine for myself that I enjoyed inside the house. After we were awakened with a different song each day, everyone would get ready and try to take advantage of the hour we were given for hot showers. I'd go to make my morning coffee, sit in the same chair in the same corner each morning, and have a cup of Turkish coffee. One of the tenants would sometimes come and chat with me, and sometimes I was just there alone with my thoughts. Once all the hot water ran out and the tenants would go out into the yard, I'd go wash my face and make time for my morning exercise. I'd go on a run of 30-60 minutes each morning for 86 days. The yard was about 40 meters in diameter (production once gave us a tape measure and I measured its diameter). I ran in circles at a slow and steady pace, hundreds of laps each time. I'd then perform power drills and go into the heated pool. This was my morning routine, how I filled up my empty mornings. It would take up to about three hours.

Once I finished my exercise and had a cool shower, I'd talk to the other tenants for a bit and then read the only book in the house – the Bible. I read the entire Bible. We'd often read it together and analyze the stories. They later also brought the New Testament into the house, since a Christian tenet named

Paul had come in, and I read it as well. I felt that I'd defeated boredom, the greatest enemy on that show.

I remember losing my sense of time at a certain point. I'd gotten so used to it that I thought this was what the rest of my life would look like. A part of my brain realized it was wrong, but another part was so used to it that I actually felt like being inside the *Big Brother* house was real life. Another thing happened that disturbed me at first, though I later embraced it. I missed my family and friends tremendously during the first few weeks. My desire to see anyone familiar, even if for a few moments, was the peak of my passion and dreams. But after a few weeks, I no longer missed them. I simply stopped missing my family and friends. My brain went through a process of accepting rather than forgetting. There was no life outside, only inside the house.

The tenants nominated me for eviction almost every week, mostly due to a small group that made sure to remind me of my political opinions. Surprisingly, and much to the surprise of the rest of the tenants as well, the audience made sure to keep me on the show, week in and week out. The first few times, I thought it was a coincidence, but I later realized there were quite a few people at home who related to what I was trying to say. You're completely cut off from the outside world while on *Big Brother*, it's like you're on Mars and can't communicate with Earth, and the evictions are the only message you can get from the outside. The only other message you could get was that every few days, there would be some people gathered at the "shouting hill" next to where the house was located, and they would shout or use megaphones. After a few weeks there, I heard a wonderful group of people shouting my name for the first time. I was embarrassed yet simultaneously proud and happy. People had actually left their homes to shout my name, express their support. It was a very sweet moment. When the show was over, I met with those wonderful women who made sure to come cheer me on; I had a hard time explaining to them just how much they'd bolstered my spirits while I was there. Another highlight was when a helicopter appeared in the sky with a poster supporting me. The helicopter had a big sign that read: "Nir, whether Left or Right, we love you and are proud of you! Your family, friends and supporters." These were the moments in which I understood that the big risk I had taken was worth it.

I had good experiences. All in all, I felt positive and safe throughout the time I spent in the *Big Brother* house.

One week, the producers decided that celebrities would play the role of *Big Brother* for two days, meaning they'd control the house. The first was singer Dana International, and then they brought someone I never thought they'd return to the show: Oren Hazan. Again. This time not as a tenant, but above me. I was again angry at the producers, not understanding why they were bringing him back to primetime. After a while, Oren called me to the *Big Brother* room. I went in, not knowing why. What happened there was never broadcast. We almost immediately got into quite a low argument. At some point Oren got annoyed and told me that our conversation was over, and that the minute I stepped out he'd play the national anthem on the house speakers, to see how I felt about it. At the beginning of the show, I mentioned that I hadn't sung the national anthem in recent years, out of solidarity with the Arab minority in the country, because I believe the anthem should represent all the country's citizens. Oren knew that. I knew being in the house during the national anthem would be 'an extermination zone', and too complicated a situation to intently explain to the tenants – certainly to the viewers – and I knew it would be unfairly used outside the house, surely without giving me the opportunity to explain myself. One of the first things you learn in the Officers' Course is to identify where the enemy has set up the 'extermination zone' and to avoid it; once you enter, you'll probably get exterminated. I understood that I had lost once I left the room. I was on the show for long enough to understand how things worked, and where the production's weak spots were. I told Oren I wasn't leaving the room, and I also demanded that Roy – the show's chief editor – come talk to me. Oren said there was no way that would happen. I knew Roy was next to him, that it was all a game, but I also knew I was holding up the entire show. I sat there for a long time, not sure how long, 30 minutes or even an hour. Oren was enraged, I could hear it in his voice. They eventually gave in. Roy, who was furious at me, started talking to me. I explained the situation and made him promise that Oren wouldn't do what he was planning on doing. I agreed to come out only after getting an explicit promise. Roy gave me what I asked for, but demanded that I not talk to the rest of the tenants. I left upset, but on the other hand, felt I'd escaped a situation that could've been very poorly interpreted. Happily, as I later watched the episode, I saw that Oren was once again seen in a bad light, and understood why it was important for them to have him back on the show.

I was on *Big Brother* for 86 days, and was evicted about 9 days before the finale. I had survived seven eliminations, meaning the audience at home had decided to let me off the hook seven times. I left a winner. I felt that I had contributed to the country's political left, in however small a way, but I'd entered a slot many similar people had failed in before me, on a show many of them had no wish to be on, and I'd succeeded. It wasn't a personal success for me, as Nir Avishai Cohen, but success as a representative of the section that was never nominated. I started the show with very low success rates, a candidate certain for early eviction, and managed to survive that lion's den without compromising my opinions, without having to apologize; on the contrary, I'd left with my head held high and at peace with my opinions and my way – I'd even managed to get some messages across to Israeli society.

Among the many things that excited me was the love and support I received from Israeli society. I got thousands of messages and comments from men and women of the Arab denomination who supported me and the messages I conveyed. Of all the channels and newspapers that invited me over, I was happiest for the interview with "Hala TV", the most-watched channel in the Arab community.

Sure, there were some negative reactions, quite a few of them. I even got death threats – on social media as well – and was cursed in public. One time, someone actually threatened me on the street. I went to the police, and filed charges twice. I knew they wouldn't do anything about it, but I also wanted to send a message: I lovingly accept criticism but won't tolerate violence. I was repeatedly asked why I didn't delete bad comments and curses from my Instagram posts; it was because to me, these comments are part of Israeli society and reflect the atmosphere towards people who hold on different opinions, and everyone should acknowledge that. I don't want to blur out or beautify reality. One day I was walking down the Tel Aviv promenade and someone suddenly came at me, starting to curse me. He threatened to stab me in the guts for being a "traitor leftist". Before I even got a chance to react, he turned around and left. That's what an incited person looks like. I have no doubt this person is a result of everything that was going on online back then. There were so many toxic posts against me, so many shockingly violent comments, but most of the comments were positive and reinforcing. Fifteen minutes of fame are real – right after I came out of *Big Brother*, a flattering article was published about me in the weekend edition of Yedioth Ahronoth's newspaper *Shiva Leylot*. I also had a positive interview on Channel 13's early news, and a long interview with journalist Hila Korah just before the *Big Brother* finale on primetime TV. These two interviews allowed me to convey the ideas that had caused me to come onto the show in the first place.

There were other ripples from being famous: thousands of people asking to take selfies with me, gossip columns publishing endless flattering segments... I received offers to collaborate for fees or gifts (I refused most of them), daily invitations to go on the radio or TV, thousands of support posts on social media and even fan gatherings, and mostly a lot of support from people on the street. All in all, it was a very positive sensation.

A day after I went into the *Big Brother* house, a famous Israeli rapper – an influential figure on the right, with hundreds of thousands of social media followers – wrote that I was the most dangerous person in the country at that time. He understood what it meant to have a left-wing person on primetime that might – God forbid – be seen positively and might have young people listening to him, and perhaps absorbing a democratic value or two rather than the inciting propaganda he'd been promoting for years. Truth be told? I now understand why he wrote that, and he was right to do so. The thousands of messages I received from young people confirmed the worst as far as he and others on the right believed. Some young people were exposed to democratic content by following the show, and started criticizing right-wing propaganda, Maybe not all Arabs wanted to kill Jews; maybe security-wise and financially Israel would be better off not being present in the Territories; maybe settlements were damaging the country's security rather than defending it.

Most of all, I was glad there were a few young people who were willing to listen, and have a conversation.

The thing that convinced me to go into a house full of cameras for three months, without a shred of privacy, was the thought that there was no way our values wouldn't be presented on primetime, mainly in front of young people. I wanted to talk about what was considered taboo in Israeli society. I wanted to fight for my right to express my opinion (and voice it for others who identified with it), in the belief that justice lay on my side of the fence. And if that justice had to be spoken out while wearing a frozen chicken suit or a cardboard costume, that was what I'd do. Perhaps this is my greatest insight from this experience: what's the point of justice if it's not made accessible? And yes, if exposing young people to the left-wing section of society, not to mention the democratic section, means wallowing into the primetime swamp, then while you can debate the quality of what's considered a national campfire – which is how I refer to *Big Brother* – you can't ignore the fact that it's what many of the young people consume.

There's one thing that has to be said: the leftists are losing the younger generation. Pessimists would say we've lost an entire generation of teenagers and people in their 20s. I see it in the average age at the demonstrations, in the people who show up for tours with human rights movements, but most of all I see it in the age range of people who write and comment on social media. Very few young people speak up in favor of the left compared to the multitudes of those who echo the populist slogans of the right. This is where things stand, and we have to look reality in the face.

I often hear young people on my side say: "What difference does it make? What's the point of fighting? We've already lost."

The reality is that there's a vast majority of slogan-spewers from the right on primetime, and have been for a long time now. Fear and incitement rule. Israeli reality became black or white: left equals bad and right equals good.

It's that simple. Any other opinion or viewpoint is met with incitement and silencing. A democratic society has to have multiplicities of opinions, and allow us to discuss them. But these discussions no longer take place on the popular platforms that young people use. Yes, a good article in a left-wing-associated newspaper is an important thing, but what happens everywhere else? How many young people actually read these articles? Most of the youth's public opinion leaders are afraid to say anything about human rights, not to mention the word "occupation" at a show, in a song or even in an interview.

Let there be no mistakes, I'm not naïve. I don't think that three months on *Big Brother* changed things around, I don't think the left will resurrect upon my appearance there. But I do think it holds a few insights about the current situation and the future of the sector in Israel that believes in democracy.

Perhaps if a few more famous people who are more widely heard – mostly among younger people – broke the silence and echoed the values of this side of the country, it'd be more legitimate to specifically voice politically leftist opinions, and have discussions in general.

While I only added a toothpick to the campfire, it was on a national level.

Chapter Eleven

And After All That – Possible Solutions

The way I see it, one of the greatest tragedies of the Israeli occupation, as far as Israeli citizens are concerned, is the fact we can live a complete life in Israel without feeling it, without even actually knowing it exists. After all, for the average citizen – one who doesn't dive into the matter, and at best watches the news every now and again – there's no occupation. The image, decisively shown in news channels and media is that there's a conflict between Israel and the Palestinians; a bloody conflict in which, most often, the Palestinians are obviously the "bad guys" who chose the path of war, who are trying to murder us, and who are happy for every spilled drop of Israeli blood. We have forgotten to separate terrorists from the majority of Palestinians, who are people – just like us – simple people who want to live in peace, raise families and enjoy the simplicity of life, just like everyone else.

A long-lasting conflict can only exist on the basis of ignorance and false information. **Alongside the immense project to expand the settlements, another project began planting the seeds of false and misleading information in the national consciousness, making it the main narrative of**

Israeli citizens. On top of this false information, the settlers and their supporters are busy inciting and blurring everything that actually happens in the Territories. By the way, this is where the false and poisonous propaganda started – and still continues – against human rights organizations that act against the occupation. These same organizations are mostly concerned with exposing the truth which composes the big picture of reality, so they can open our eyes to one simple value: peace and camaraderie between people. But the big picture is dangerous for those who seek to maintain the Israeli sin in the Territories.

In 2019, when Israel hosted the Eurovision, a "Breaking the Silence" campaign called for overseas tourists to visit Hebron. Among other things, the ad was published on a huge billboard over Ayalon Highway. The ad had two images on it, one of Tel Aviv's great beaches and the other the Territories' West Bank Barrier. The ad was in English, inviting tourists to see the big picture. There was rage once again: how dare "Breaking the Silence" invite tourists to see what the country was looking to hide? This is exactly what the country's been trying to do for many years, in full view of the entire Israeli society. Israel doesn't want us to talk about its backyard, where it carries out all its wrongs, only our beautiful façade: the great and liberal Tel Aviv, the holy city of Jerusalem, the Dead Sea and the exciting north. We 'dare not mention the Territories.

'For over twenty years the "Taglit – Birthright Israel" project has been bringing Jews from all over the world to Israel. The project's website says that its goal is to "strengthen the Jewish identity of young Jewish adults and create a foundation for ongoing Jewish connection. They'll go on a 10-day educational tour of the country, along with Israeli soldiers and students, and together they'll get to know the young and vibrant Israel."

Over 500,000 young Jewish people have arrived in Israel following this project, with thousands of these tours to get to know Israel. These young people travel the entire country except for one area – the country's backyard. The young people from Birthright usually don't visit the West Bank (Judea and Samaria). Some would say 'this is for security reasons, but I have no doubt that's not the truth. The people of Birthright also know that anyone with democratic values would have a lot of questions and probably criticize the situation in the Territories. The reality of the Territories certainly wouldn't strengthen the connection with Israel, and isn't a part of the "young and vibrant Israel." In the spirit of the Israeli government, the people of Birthright also simply choose to hide the Territories from these young Jewish people's eyes and awareness.

The Israeli government simply doesn't want people to know what's going on in the Territories, since they know it's wrong and immoral, certainly undemocratic. Thus, the establishment – which wishes to maintain the status quo – does everything in its power to attack and silence those who wish to expose that reality to Israeli society and the world; all is fair in war, even turning people who love this country into anti-Israeli traitors.

In every lecture I give to pre-military academy students, I'm amazed at how much they don't know. These same young people are the product of an education system that makes sure not to tell them, makes sure they'll know nothing 'beyond the false narrative they've been trying to tell for so many years. I always have cadets coming to me at the end of each lecture, telling me that regardless of whether they agree with me or not, they've never heard the point of view I've mentioned about the Territories.

These lines have been written so I can reach more people, create another crack – even a small one – in the wall of concealment built in Israel, which divides the reality of the Territories and the vast majority of its citizens, who don't actually know what reality looks like in that shared land.

I've been asked many times – by friends and strangers alike – that if I'm so critical of this country, why do I still live here? I have a European passport, I can live anywhere I want in Europe, in much more democratic surroundings, and I can live a better life. First of all, I have no doubt that I'm currently a minority in my own country, and unfortunately a small minority at that. But just because you're part of a minority doesn't mean that justice is not on your side. There are countless cases in history where minorities fought for justice, and became the majority. I'm not going anywhere, because 'firstly this is my country – for better or worse. This is where I was born, this is where my family is, this is where I've made my home. I'm part of a sector struggling for its home, for the current and future face of this country. My dear father keeps saying, every chance he gets, that he doesn't know how or when, but he doesn't doubt the occupation will one day end. I agree with him, but I also think it will come thanks to people who won't stop fighting for it. Millions of Palestinians suffer every single day due to the current situation in the Territories, which is another reason I'm not leaving; I feel responsible for my Palestinian brothers and sisters. I take responsibility for my actions, and my country's actions, and I won't forget it. Practically speaking, I could easily immigrate, but I think I shouldn't, that it would be immoral. We, this tiny sector, have to keep fighting for all people living in the area stretching from the Jordan River to the Mediterranean Sea. I want to see the State of Israel prosper, and I also want to see a Palestinian state prosper alongside it. At the end of the day, people are people. I feel that as an Israeli citizen, I have a responsibility toward all Palestinians as well as the next generation of Israelis growing up in this country.

I believe in peace, a word that will soon be forgotten in the Hebrew vocabulary. Peace between people, between countries. But my current leaders won't do anything to promote this peace; they can afford not to do so because hardly anyone demands it of them anymore.

One of our worst issues as a society is our political indifference, especially from the younger generations. The ones who should have the most interest when it comes to the future of this country are in their twenties, the ones who are supposed to live here for many more years. Strangely enough, it's those young people who are indifferent to the current state of affairs, as if this is a decree from on high, as if it's none of their business – the politicians will decide as they will. The most politically-involved people around the world are students, they are the ones who lead protests, who make change happen. And here in Israel, escapism is king: most young people stay away from politics as if it were fire, especially on the left. The first time I saw a glimmer of hope was during the Balfour protest, but the fire went out a year later. Unfortunately, there's no continuity with that same great protest of young people, and we weren't smart enough to translate it into political power. Same parties, almost the same exact politicians. There's a brilliant politician here and there, like Na'ama Lazimi from the Labor Party, but she's an exception who doesn't prove the rule.

Albert Einstein said that "Insanity is doing the same thing over and over again, expecting a different result." This is exactly what the left is doing: they keep repeating the same action over and over again, the worn-out Meretz party or Labor trying to escape the left and dreaming of becoming a centrist party. The left must undergo a change in order for anything else to happen here, and I see two major changes that can offset the political equation and even the political state.

The first change that must take place here is more female political involvement, specifically female dominance in politics and running the country's affairs. Men have been running Israeli politics for too long, controlling the country, and they hold all key positions. It's time for women to lead this country. Women would think differently, run the country with wisdom and feminine creativity. Not just one or two women as tokens, but a party with a female majority. Women should set the tone. Sure, there will still be men in politics, but I believe real change will come when women are the political majority and hold key positions. Ex-generals have been running this country for too long; some were good at their military careers, others weren't. These ex-generals won't try anything new; they keep doing the same thing: they maintain a masculine, military culture that believes in force and unimaginative solutions.

The other change that must take place is the establishment of a Jewish-Arab party. It's not just the future of the left but the future of the entire Israeli democracy that lies in the sociopolitical unification of Jews and Arabs. A party that gives equal representation to both Jews and Arabs, that serves as a political representation for those who believe in cohabitation within the State of Israel, could lead to a significant change in the country. The left has to shuffle its deck, erase its current parties and create something new, a new leadership. Joint Arab-Jewish leadership, female leadership, could shift Israel back to its democratic lines. This is a move that will shake local politics, break the existing structure and place a new one in its stead, truer and much healthier.

Many may not know this, but the Oslo Accords – the agreement signed in 1993 following the peace talks between Israelis and Palestinians – were initially set for five years, after which a permanent solution should have been signed. This temporary status, which has lasted for almost thirty years, was not drawn up for that long a period. Both sides initially wanted to stop the violence between the two peoples, and give the Palestinians initial autonomy. The wave of terror attacks, along with the assassination of Prime Minister Yitzhak Rabin, stopped that positive process. I object to the statement that the Oslo Accords were a mistake. On the contrary, they started a true and positive process of peace between the peoples, after a bloody century of conflict.

Examining the Oslo Accords on their own, without understanding that they were only the beginning of the process, is stupidity and a lack of understanding at best, and an attempt to rewrite reality at worst, making Israeli society remember them as a grave mistake and using them to prevent any real peace treaty between Israel and the Palestinians. Unfortunately, the latter is a common belief. Following the assassination of Yitzhak Rabin and the right's rise to power (in fact, other than the two years of Ehud Barak's tenure as Prime Minister, and as of the writing of these passages, there have only been right-wing governments in power in Israel, including the Bennet-Lapid government, those who believe in the settlements project became even more influential in Parliament. The result was a series of very successful mind-altering campaigns insisting the Palestinians did not wish for peace, and that the only solution that could protect the State of Israel was to establish more and more settlements. This is probably the biggest lie in the history and narratives of Israeli society. As I've mentioned before, the settlements are doing the exact opposite, endangering the State of Israel, and furthermore, the settlers are endangering IDF soldiers. Our military and civilian cemeteries are full of soldiers and civilians who died at the altar of this lie. As long as settlements exist, we cannot form a clear border between us and the Palestinians, thus it's impossible to allow the security forces to properly defend against terrorists trying to infiltrate the sovereignty of the State of Israel. Should a Palestinian wish to cross over into Israel illegally, they are easily able to do so, without having to go through any of the IDF checkpoints. According to official statistics, tens of thousands of Palestinians illegally cross into Israel for work every day without going through the checkpoints, with the government turning a blind eye. The settlements' positioning deep within Palestinian territory requires the IDF to spread its soldiers throughout the West Bank, which makes them much more vulnerable to violent acts committed against them.

The settlements prevent us from creating a real border between Israel and the Palestinians – whether under a treaty or not – which puts Israeli citizens in even more danger within their sovereign territory. It's not just me who says this, it also comes from countless ex-generals who served as regional commanders, Chiefs of Staff, and heads of the Shin Bet. In the all-important movie *The Gatekeepers* (Shomrei HaSaf), six former heads of the Shin Bet – who cannot be accused of a lack of knowledge or loyalty to their country – clearly speak of the security-related need to separate themselves from the Palestinians, and the danger that lies in our ongoing military control of the West Bank. There are many others in their field who share these beliefs.

The human rights actions against martial law in the Territories are the ones defending the soldiers, among other things. **Anyone who claims the IDF has to be present in the Territories is endangering the soldiers in vain, disrespecting the blood of soldiers and civilians who are being killed as a result of that.** Only the revered and far-fetched Israeli reality can flip this equation around: those who send soldiers to die superfluous deaths are branded as Israel-sympathizers who care for soldiers, while the people actually taking care of them and their safety are branded anti-Israel and anti-IDF. It's enough to see who my greatest critics have been in recent years to understand my claim: people who wrote abundantly against me, claimed that I hate soldiers and act against the country, but what did they contribute to the country's security? How many of them have served as combatants in regular and Reserve service? When was the last time they put on these olive-colored uniforms and actively protected the country? The answer is clear, most of them don't. Most of them don't serve in the Reserves and don't defend the country's security. All they do is write posts about how much they love the soldiers. That's it. Where do they get the nerve, the audacity to claim these things against me? Unlike them, I've been actively protecting this country since I was eighteen years old; unlike them, I've fought in real battles and lost some of my best friends. I don't just love this country in words, I also prove it day in and day out through my actions. Looking at politics, you can see the same thing: those who are allegedly the greatest IDF sympathizers and constantly speak in favor of these soldiers are the ones who have mostly never held a weapon in their lives.

It's important for me to stress that I'm not claiming non-IDF combatants aren't allowed to voice their opinions. A person's military service has nothing to do with their right to a certain political opinion, or the legitimacy of said opinion. The discussion can't revolve around what that person has contributed to the country's security, but I am against the phenomenon of people presuming to represent a certain value – such as being IDF and Israel-sympathizers – so they can attack combatants such as my friends and I, while they haven't done a fraction of what we have.

How has MP Bezalel Smotrich, Chairman of the National Union (HaIhud HaLeumi), contributed to Israel's security? The man who constantly attacks human rights organizations and talks about the country's security? Smotrich was drafted at the age of 28 and served for 16 months at IDF Headquarters in Tel Aviv (HaKirya). MP Itamar Ben-Gvir, another representative of the extreme right and the Settlers, hasn't even served in the military for so much as a single day. That same Ben-Gvir who's even been convicted of criminal charges, including interference with a police officer and charges of supporting a terror organization. But in this warped reality, the people I've just mentioned – who have nothing or very little for the country's security, and certainly weren't combatants – are considered the country's greatest sympathizers and being pro-IDF soldiers, while people like me, Avner Gvaryahu (CEO of "Breaking the Silence", who served as a combatant in the Paratroopers' "Orev" anti-tank unit) and Achiya Schatz (my boss at "Breaking the Silence", who served as a combatant in "Duvdevan") are considered traitors and anti-IDF by many people in this country. I can't hate IDF soldiers because I am, as of the fifth decade of my life, an IDF soldier. Had I thought the IDF was fundamentally immoral, I certainly wouldn't still serve in its ranks. I do think the IDF is being sent to carry out immoral acts in the Territories. But once again, I'm not against IDF soldiers. My claims are aimed at those who send them there, meaning the government and those who elect it, we citizens. An uneven equation has been created, as if no matter how much you've contributed to the country's security, once you've opposed the occupation you're automatically tagged as anti-Israeli. We can't agree to this equation.

Approximately 15 million people live between the Jordan River and the Mediterranean Sea, meaning Israeli territory, the West Bank, and the Gaza Strip. 10 million Israelis, more than 2 million of whom are Arab (most of them defining themselves as Palestinians); 3 million Palestinians in the West Bank, and about 2 million more in the Gaza Strip. This means half of the population in Israel and the Territories are Jewish Israelis, and the other half are Muslim Palestinians (all data is approximate).

I see three options for the future of the people on this

aforementioned piece of land:

One, which is unfortunately becoming less realistic – even though I think it's best – is the good old two-state solution. The State of Israel alongside the State of Palestine, following an exchange of territory and setting clear borders between them.

There's no need to elaborate on the solution because it exists. Those who wish to see its details can go to the Geneva Initiative's website – it's all there.

At the start of the 2000s, former senior members of the Israeli and Palestinian societies worked on a peace treaty between the two sides. Everything was agreed upon, all the issues, and written up. There is a consensus about it – should the parties decide to go for a two-state solution, the Geneva Initiative would serve as the outline for the agreement.

I support this solution. I respect the national ambitions of the Palestinian people, and just as the State of Israel is the home of the Jewish people and all its citizens, so should the State of Palestine be the home of the Palestinian people.

Instead of wasting both people's energies and resources on a terrible conflict, we can have peace and tranquility that will lead the area to prosper. If you need examples, look to the Sinai evacuation. We also evacuated Israeli settlements from there, though the Egyptians were our bitter enemies then, and there has been a peaceful border between the two countries for over forty years, with joint interests in the war on terror, and of course Sinai and Eilat as desirable touristic destinations. These are the fruits of peace. Working at the Israeli embassy in Cairo, living there, and my long-standing service at the Egyptian border made this realization clearer, I saw it before my eyes and still do. Some tried to frighten us back then, that if we gave back the Sinai Peninsula Egyptian tanks would gallop toward Eilat on their way to conquer Tel Aviv. There were also doomsday prophecies back then which turned out to be complete nonsense.

Another example: back in 1982, the IDF invaded Lebanon as part of the first Lebanon War, and after another terrible war Israel decided that the IDF would remain there in what was referred to as "southern Lebanon". They perceived that the IDF had to rule that area in order to defend the northern settlements of Israel. More than 600 IDF soldiers were killed on the altar of this security prospect, for about 18 years. In all that time, the northern settlements suffered constant missile launches, especially in the northern city of Kiryat Shmona. But the doomsday prophecies said there was no choice, that the northern settlements would never be safe if the IDF pulled out of southern Lebanon. The "Four Mothers" movement challenged that false equation and started a public struggle against the IDF's redundant presence there and in favor of retreating to an international border. Following massive public pressure, then-Prime Minister Ehud Barak bravely withdrew the IDF forces to the international border in 2000. Until the publication of this book in 2023, aside from one month during the second Lebanon War, the northern border has remained quiet. This is despite the fact that the Hezbollah, a terror organization much stronger than Hamas or any other terror organization around Israel, is on the other side of that border.

I mention these two withdrawals – Sinai and southern Lebanon – because false prophets predicted the worst in both cases.

These prophecies sowed fear in the hearts of Israeli citizens, that the country would be doomed if we went through with the plans.

Those prophecies turned out to be false.

Those prophecies are given on a daily basis by those same people regarding the evacuation of settlements and the establishment of the Palestinian state. Once again, the same use of fear, the same threats of death and destruction. The same people who scared us then continue to do so today. These people don't want peace, they believe in the way of war and are willing to sacrifice IDF soldiers in vain.

I'm often asked about the Gaza Strip. "That's an example of a place we withdrew from, and have been constantly bombarded since." Again, that false narrative is spread by the right. First, some facts: in the five years prior to the withdrawal from Gush Katif (the detachment), 124 Israeli were killed; 39 of them civilians, and 85 members of the armed forces. Back then there were many missiles fired at the city of Sderot. Add to the data of these five years the thousands of wounded and slain Palestinians. Those who try and pass off that time, before the withdrawal, as being quiet are simply lying. Countless soldiers died during Israel's presence at Gush Katif, in vain. Yes, we pulled back from Gaza, and we did well in this. Instead of reaching a political agreement with the leaders of the Strip, Israel turned Gaza into one big prison. The Gaza Strip is the worst place in the world to live in, with several hours of electricity a day, without adequate infrastructure or medical services. Once again Israel's false perception is that its military force would solve the conflict. Gaza won't go away, and its people won't stand for living in subhuman conditions forever. The violent rounds in Gaza only conclusively proved one thing: they're simply no help. Rivers of blood have been shed in Gaza, and insane destruction wrought, yet millions of people still live there. Solving Gaza can only be achieved through some kind of political agreement. Offering Gaza as an example of a failed withdrawal is a terrible mistake. Awful leadership has been dragging the Gaza issue out for over fifteen years; those suffering are firstly the Palestinians who live there, but also the Israelis in the Gaza Envelope. Israel has tried everything with the people of Gaza except for one thing, a political agreement that would lead to a peace treaty with the Palestinians. By the way, it's clear to everyone that a peace treaty with the Palestinians would include the territories of the West Bank and Gaza Strip together, and the connection of these territories. The connection would take place in what's called the "safe passage". Once again, all the details are already included in the Geneva Initiative agreement.

The second solution is one country spanning the entire area. This solution is twofold:

First, Israel will remain a democratic country, officially annexing all the territories of the West Bank and the Gaza Strip, and sustaining one country for both people. In this option, all the country's citizens are given citizenship, obviously including voting rights. This solution isn't realistic as far as I see it, certainly not in the short run, for two reasons. The first is that the Palestinians will never agree to it because of their national aspiration for a state of their own; the second is Israelis won't stand for it because it basically means the end of the State of Israel as a Jewish state. I'm personally not against this solution, as long as it's jointly agreed upon by both Palestinians and Israelis.

The second option for the one-state solution is that Israel annexes the territories of the West Bank, but won't give residential status to the Palestinian population. This solution will transform Israel from a democratic country that imposes martial law in the Territories into an official apartheid state, meaning a regime that openly has two sets of laws and rights for two populations living in the same area and state. I'm obviously against this solution, and I think the world would be too. In other words, I don't think this option is realistic either.

The third solution for the status quo is what's happening now. This is the solution the State of Israel has been promoting for the past twenty years, with the support of the settlers. This means turning this temporary situation into a permanent one. This solution means the settlements will remain and so will martial law in the Territories, without annexation, while using the Palestinian Authority as the entity that takes care of the municipal needs of the Palestinian people. I believe this is a very bad option, and it's what I'm fighting to stop.

This option is bad for both peoples.

The only ones who gain from this are the settlers, who continue to feed off the national treasury and expand the vast settlement project they've built.

In this current state, Israel's security remains vulnerable, IDF soldiers keep endangering themselves in vain, and the Palestinians are obviously still living under martial law that deprives them of basic human rights and operates like a dictatorship.

For the past twenty years, the Israeli government has shown zero interest in resolving the Israeli-Palestinian conflict, zero interest in making peace. The Israeli government has only been interested in one thing: stalling, without any future plans, without taking care of future generations, as long as the government survives another year.

Any sensible person knows that the way things are now can't go on forever. The Palestinians won't stay oppressed forever as they watch Israel thrive financially. I have no doubt the day will come when young Palestinian people demand change, demand their freedom, and rightfully so. No army, no matter how strong, can defeat a people striving to be free. We cannot rule the Palestinians with the might of our sword forever, nor do we have any reason to do so. There's no question that the Israeli occupation of the Territories will someday end, the only question is when that happens and how much death and suffering the people living here will endure, both Israeli and Palestinians.

I believe the thing that can drive Israelis to find a solution, rather than maintain this current situation, is intervention from the outside world. The family of democratic countries cannot keep turning a blind eye to the Occupied Territories, and keep acting as if there's no occupation when dealing with Israel. International pressure, including financial sanctions on the State of Israel, could make a change, and lead Israelis to understand that they have to make a decision regarding the future of the martial law we impose upon the Palestinians. I believe that when Israeli citizens realize there's a price to the occupation, and that they're paying it on a personal level – financial losses or an inability to enter certain countries – there's a chance they'll wake up from their long-term slumber. Financial sanctions and academic and cultural boycotts can bring Israelis to a decision that will benefit their future. History shows that international pressure on South Africa was one of the leading factors in ending the apartheid regime. I believe that such pressure can also be a significant catalyst for ending the Israeli occupation.

Chapter Twelve

One Drop, Then Another

This book was inspired by the lectures I had the honor of giving to thousands of young people in recent years. I'm internationally using the word 'honored' because I got to have deep and meaningful conversations with thousands of young people, and that's a privilege not many people get. This is probably the most significant thing that came of my publicity following my appearance on that reality show.

I'm not naïve, I don't think those who listened to my viewpoint would change their minds after a 2-hour lecture. But maybe, for some of those who sat there and listened to me, I was able to form a little crack in a very specific monochromatic narrative that paints an entire wing in a problematic and distancing color.

At the end of each lecture, I had students come up and talk to me. There's one powerful statement that keeps repeating itself: *I still don't know if I agree with you, but it's the first time I've heard that perspective. You've given me food for thought.* This is exactly that crack I'm aiming for, making these young people ask questions, wonder, and doubt.

That's also how I finish each of my lectures. After a long

conversation, I ask to add one more thing. I ask these young people to question things, to not accept anything for granted, as fate. I ask them to check, explore and ask, to have conversations with themselves and their friends about anything, mostly about what seems like absolute truths. Thanks to these lectures, I've realized how problematic the future of the left in Israel really is. If we keep operating in the same way, we won't be able to win over new people; public opinion will stay as is, we'll continue to be a minority and nothing will change in the Israeli reality. There are no magic tricks that will change Israeli public opinion – it's a long way to go, which I believe starts with education. The content Israeli students receive and the places the education system refers its students to, and a meaningful representation of leftist beliefs everywhere young people are being taught, whether youth movements, pre-military boarding schools or National Service. We have to be present and have an effect everywhere, especially in educational institutions where there are young people who aren't yet politically set, just before they go to vote for the first time in their lives, a vote that can influence their future first and foremost.

A society that doesn't evolve, doesn't change, and is stagnant is a sick society, one that won't last. I greatly believe in the opportunity to change and hope for a better future. But this better future will only come if we put in the effort today.

My contribution to this better and different future may be extremely limited, just a drop in the ocean. As Arik Einstein's song goes: "I only wanted to put a drop in. Because one drop, then another, and another after that, will turn it into an ocean[25]."

---

25   From the song "One Drop" by Arik Einstein.

On the other side of the world, perhaps there of all places, some things get clearer, taking shape and being put into words. I was traveling in Central America while writing this book. At the end of the second day of my four-day trip, after an excruciating climb of 1,500 meters and many kilometers of walking, we arrived at our destination: a tiny village in the mountains of Guatemala, 3,200 meters above sea level. A few houses, no electricity, no running water, with only foot access. We lit a fire to keep warm and cooked what little food we had. There were four of us: a lovely French couple, the great local guide and I.

We started talking about songs, and the guide asked me to sing Israel's national anthem. I replied that I hadn't sung the national anthem in years, and that it posed an issue for me. He made an understanding face, but probably didn't. Right after, he asked the French couple to sing their national anthem and they did so with great pride. It was a magical moment I just had to catch on film: citizens being proud of their country.

At that moment, as I was documenting their singing, a few tears ran down my cheek. They were tears of jealousy, as I was jealous of their pride, but also tears of sadness. I felt like the son of a criminal, who loves his father but is ashamed of his actions. There, at the end of the world, it all became clearer. I love my country and always will, but it's been too long since I was proud of being an Israeli. I don't sing the anthem because I'm not proud of the hideous crimes of the occupation, not proud of marginalizing the Palestinian minority that lives in this country, and not proud of the racism. I love my country, but I'm not proud of it.

I long for that moment when I'll be proud of Israel, when I can walk the world and proudly say I'm Israeli. I believe this day will come; good will ultimately prevail.